Selected Poems: John Montague

page 73

BOOKS BY JOHN MONTAGUE

poetry

Poisoned Lands
A Chosen Light
Tides
The Rough Field
A Slow Dance
The Great Cloak
The Dead Kingdom

short stories

Death of a Chieftain

editor

The Book of Irish Verse

John Montague

SELECTED
POEMS

Wake Forest University Press

Wake Forest University Press

Copyright © John Montague, 1982, 1991.

Designed and printed on Zephyr Antique Laid by The Porcupine's
Quill (Erin, Ontario) for Exile Editions (Toronto). Published in
the United States of America by Wake Forest University Press,
Winston-Salem, North Carolina 27109. The type is Stempel
Garamond.

The cover is after a colour etching by S.W. Hayter.

The drawing on page 7 is by Louis le Brocquy.

Library of Congress Catalogue Number 81-71131

ISBN 0-916390-15-2 (paper)

for Barry Callaghan

PART I

IRISH STREET SCENE, WITH LOVERS

A rainy quiet evening, with leaves that hang
Like squares of silk from dripping branches.
An avenue of laurel, and the guttering cry
Of a robin that balances a moment,
Starts and is gone
On some furtive errand of its own.

A quiet evening, with skies washed and grey;
A tiredness as though the day
Swayed towards sleep,
Except for the reserved statement
Of rain on the stone-grey pavement –
Dripping, they move through this marine light,

Seeming to swim more than walk,
Linked under the black arch of an umbrella,
With its assembly of spokes like points of stars,
A globule of water slowly forming on each.
The world shrinks to the soaked, worn
Shield of cloth they parade beneath.

1952

SPEECH FOR AN IDEAL IRISH ELECTION

Then the visionary lady
Walked like a magician's daughter
Across green acres of Ireland;
The broad bright sword
Of the politician's word
Summoned applause in every square.

The unseen inhabited
A well, a corner of a field;
Houses assumed magic light
From patriots' memory;
Assemblies knelt in awe before
The supernatural in a shaking tree.

The light that never was
Enlarged profile, gun and phrase:
Green of the grass worn
On shoulder as catalytic token;
Acrid speech of rifle and gun
Easing neurosis into definite action.

The house subsides into stillness,
Buried bombs ignore the spade.
The evening light, suitably grave,
Challenges renewed activity.
The transfigured heroes assume
Grey proportions of statuary.

Now the extraordinary hour of calm
And day of limitation.
The soft grasses stir
Where unfinished dreams
Are buried with the Fianna
In that remote rock cave.

Who today asks for more
— Smoke of battle blown aside —
Than the struggle with casual
Graceless unheroic things,
The greater task of swimming
Against a slackening tide?

CALEDON CASTLE

That was my first glimpse of opulence;
A line of peacocks deployed upon the lawn
Before a wide-windowed house.
And I was five and clutched a larger hand,
Marvelling how the marvellous birds
Expanded their wild tails like fans.
Under the warm trees, the deer grazed,
Under the walls, the peacocks strayed,
Under the windows, stone fountains played,
In a doomed and formal dance of opulence.

THE ANSWER

for Christopher Ricks

How when one entered a cottage
to ask directions, the woman of the house
rose to greet you, not as a stranger
but a visitor:
                    that was the old way,
the way of courtesy.
                              Searching for Gallarus,
I crossed a half-door on the Dingle peninsula
and stood tasting the neat silence
of the swept flags, the scoured delft
on the tall dresser where even something
tinny like a two-legged, horned alarm-clock
was isolated into meaning;
                                    while friendly,
unafraid, the woman turned her face
like a wrinkled windfall, to proffer
the ritual greetings:
                          Dia dhuit/
Dia agus Muire dhuit/
                              Dia agus Muire
*agus Padraig dhuit**
                          invocation of powers
to cleanse the mind.
                          Then the question
and the answer.
                    'What did she say?'
I was asked when I came back to the car
but could only point the way
over the hill to where
                              obscured in sea
mist, the small, grey stones of the oratory
held into the Atlantic for a thousand years.

* Literally: God (Mary and Patrick) to you.

A FOOTNOTE ON MONASTICISM:
DINGLE PENINSULA

In certain places, still, surprisingly, you come
Upon them, resting like old straw hats set down
Beside the sea, weather-beaten but enduring
For a dozen centuries: here the mound
That was the roof has slithered in
And the outlines you can barely trace:
Nor does it matter since every wilderness
Along this coast retains more signs
In ragged groupings of these cells and caves,
Of where the hermits, fiercely dispossessed,
Found refuge among gulls and rocks
The incessant prayer of nearby waves.

Among darkening rocks he prayed,
Body chastened and absurd,
An earth-bound dragging space
His spirit blundered like a bird:
Hands, specialised by prayer,
Like uplifted chalices,
Nightly proffering the self
To soundless, perfect messengers.

There are times, certainly, looking through a window
At amiable clustered humanity, or scanning
The leaves of some old book, that one might wish
To join their number, start a new and fashionable
Sect beside the Celtic sea, long favourable
To dreams and dreamers; anchorites whose love
Was selfishly alone, a matter so great
That only to stone could they whisper it:
Breaking the obstinate structure of flesh
With routine of vigil and fast,
Till water-cress stirred on the palate
Like the movement of a ghost.

In ceaseless labour of the spirit,
Isolate, unblessed;
Until quietude of the senses
Announces presence of a guest;
Desolation final,
Rock within and rock without
Till from the stubborn rock of the heart
The purifying waters spurt.

1953

God watches from the cracked mirror on the wall.
God is a peeping-Tom, cat-like watches all.
When the stallion plunges, God is the rider,
With dark beard, back straight as a wall.
When I cut my hand or cheek in shaving
His blood flows and there is nothing at all
To protect me from the shadow of his redemption,
My godhead hung in text of terror on the wall.

As I pass in the street young girls cry,
Lift their light skirts and cry,
And the blackbird mocks from the cherry-tree,
Lifting its wings to cry:
'Shapeless, shapeless man in black,
What is that donkey's cross upon your back,
As the young girls lift their skirts and cry,
O! listless man in sunshine wearing black!'

It is Spring again, the trout feed,
The young sap stirs and flows like sluggish blood;
More people come to Mass and better dressed:
In the mountain I heard the sighing crack of guns
And the mirror in my hand cracked too
And ran in blood and my hands were blood
Until the burning sun came down and stood
Against my sky at three, in blood.

1955

SOLILOQUY ON A SOUTHERN STRAND

A priest, holidaying on the coast
outside Sydney, thinks nostalgically
of his boyhood in Ireland.

When I was young, it was much simpler;
I saw God standing on a local hill,
His eyes were gentle and soft birds
Sang in chorus to his voice until
My body trembled, ardent in submission.
The friar came to preach the yearly sermon
For Retreat, and cried among the flaring candles:
'O children, children, if you but knew,
'Each hair is counted, everything you do
'Offends or sweetens His five wounds!'
A priest with a harsh and tuneless voice,
Raising his brown-robed arms to cry:
'Like this candle-end, the body gutters out to die!'
Calling us all to do penance and rejoice.

Hearing the preacher speak, I knew my mind
And wished to serve, leaving the friendly farm
For years of college. At first I found it strange
And feared the boys with smoother hands and voices:
I lay awake at night, longed for home.
I heard the town boys laughing in the dark
At things that made me burn with shame,
And where the votive candles whispered into wax
Hesitantly I spoke my treasured doubts,
Conquering all my passions in your Name.
I weathered years of sameness
Until I stood before the Cathedral altar,
A burly country boy but new-made priest;
My mother watched in happiness and peace.

The young people crowd the shore now,
Rushing from Sydney, like lemmings, to the sea.
Heat plays upon the glaring cluttered beach,
Casts as in a mould my beaten head and knees.
New cars come swooping in like birds
To churn and chop the dust. A wireless,
Stuck in the sand, crackles lovesick words
As girls are roughed and raced
With whirling beach-balls in the sun.
What here avails my separate cloth,
My sober self, whose meaning contradicts
The sensual drama they enact in play?
'Hot Lips, Hot Lips', the throaty singer sighs:
A young man preens aloft and dives.

Is this the proper ending for a man?
The Pacific waves crash in upon the beach,
Roll and rise and inward stretch upon the beach.
It is December now and warm,
And yet my blood is cold, my shoulders slack;
In slow submission, I turn my body
Up to the sun, as on a rack,
Enduring comfort. In a dream,
I hear the cuckoo dance his double notes,
Among the harvest stooks like golden chessmen;
Each call, an age, a continent between.
No martyrdom, no wonder, no patent loss:
Is it for this mild ending that I
Have carried, all this way, my cross?

1956

As a child I was frightened by her
Busy with her bowl of tea in a farmhouse chimney corner,
Wrapped in a cocoon of rags and shawls.
The Lord have mercy on him,
'*Go ndeanaidh Dia trocaire ar a anam.*'
She rocked and crooned,
A doll's head mouthing under stained rafters.

'The fairies of Ireland and the fairies of Scotland
'Fought on that hill all night
'And in the morning the well ran blood.
'The dead queen was buried on that hill.
'St. Patrick passed by the cross:
'There is the mark of a footprint forever
'Where he stood to pray.'

Eyes rheumy with racial memory;
Fragments of bread soaked in brown tea
And eased between shrunken gums.
Her clothes stank like summer flax;
Watched all day as she swayed
Towards death between memories and prayers
By a farmer's child in a rough play-box.

'Mrs. McGurren had the evil eye,
'She prayed prayers on the black cow:
'It dropped there and died,
'Dropped dead in its tracks.
'She stood on the mearing and cursed the Clarkes:
'They never had a good day since,
'Fluke and bad crops and a child born strange.'

In the groove a running-down record,
Heavy with local history:
Only the scratching now, the labouring breath,
Prophecy rattling aged bones.
Age is neither knowledge nor authority,
Though it may claim both,
Weaving a litany of legends against death.

But in high summer as the hills burned with corn
I strode through golden light
To the secret spirals of the burial stone:
The grass-choked well ran sluggish red –
Not with blood but ferrous rust –
But beneath the whorls of the guardian stone
What hidden queen lay dust?

1957

According to Leabhar Gabhála, *The Book of Con-*
quests, the first invasion of Ireland was by relatives of
Noah, just before the Flood. Refused entry into the Ark,
they consulted an idol which told them to flee to Ireland.

Fleeing from threatened flood, they sailed,
Seeking the fair island, without serpent or claw;
From the deck of their hasty raft watched
The soft edge of Ireland nearward draw.

A sweet confluence of waters, a trinity of rivers,
Was their first resting place:
They unloaded the women and the sensual idol,
Guiding image of their disgrace.

Division of damsels they did there,
The slender, the tender, the dimpled, the round,
It was the first just bargain in Ireland,
There was enough to go round.

Lightly they lay and pleasured
In the green grass of that guileless place:
Ladhra was the first to die;
He perished of an embrace.

Bith was buried in a stone heap,
Riot of mind, all passion spent.
Fintan fled from the ferocious women
Lest he, too, by love be rent.

Great primitive princes of our line –
They were the first, with stately freedom,
To sleep with women in Ireland:
Soft the eternal bed they lie upon.

On a lonely headland the women assembled,
Chill as worshippers in a nave,
And watched the eastern waters gather
Into a great virile flooding wave.

THE WATER CARRIER

Twice daily I carried water from the spring,
Morning before leaving for school, and evening;
Balanced as a fulcrum between two buckets.

A bramble rough path ran to the river
Where one stepped carefully across slime-topped stones,
With corners abraded as bleakly white as bones.

At the widening pool (for washing and cattle)
Minute fish flickered as one dipped,
Circling to fill, with rust-tinged water.

The second or enamel bucket was for spring water
Which, after racing through a rushy meadow,
Came bubbling in a broken drain-pipe,

Corroded wafer thin with rust.
It ran so pure and cold, it fell
Like manacles of ice on the wrists.

One stood until the bucket brimmed
Inhaling the musty smell of unpicked berries,
That heavy greenness fostered by water.

Recovering the scene, I had hoped to stylize it,
Like the portrait of an Egyptian water-carrier:
Yet halt, entranced by slight but memoried life.

I sometimes come to take the water there,
Not as return or refuge, but some pure thing,
Some living source, half-imagined and half-real

Pulses in the fictive water that I feel.

1960

THE TROUT

Flat on the bank I parted
Rushes to ease my hands
In the water without a ripple
And tilt them slowly downstream
To where he lay, tendril light,
In his fluid sensual dream.

Bodiless lord of creation
I hung briefly above him
Savouring my own absence
Senses expanding in the slow
Motion, the photographic calm
That grows before action.

As the curve of my hands
Swung under his body
He surged, with visible pleasure.
I was so preternatually close
I could count every stipple
But still cast no shadow, until

The two palms crossed in a cage
Under the lightly pulsing gills.
Then (entering my own enlarged
Shape, which rode on the water)
I gripped. To this day I can
Taste his terror on my hands.

A DRINK OF MILK

In the girdered dark
of the byre, cattle move;
warm engines hushed
to a siding groove

before the switch flicks
down for milking.
In concrete partitions
they rattle their chains

while the farmhand eases
rubber tentacles to tug
lightly but rhythmically
on their swollen dugs

and up the pale cylinders
of the milking machine
mounts an untouched
steadily pulsing stream.

Only the tabby steals
to dip its radar whiskers
with old fashioned relish
in a chipped saucer

and before Seán lurches
to kick his boots off
in the night-silent kitchen
he draws a mug of froth

to settle on the sideboard
under the hoard of delft.
A pounding transistor shakes
the Virgin on her shelf

as he dreams towards bed.
A last glance at a magazine,
he puts the mug to his head,
grunts, and drains it clean.

Not those slim-flanked fillies
slender-ankled as models
glimpsed across the rails
through sunlong afternoons
as with fluent fetlocks
they devoured the miles

Nor at some Spring Show
a concourse of Clydesdales
waiting, huge as mammoths,
as enormous hirsute dolls,
for an incongruous rose to
blossom behind their ears

Nor that legendary Pegasus
leaping towards heaven:
only those hold my affection
who, stolid as weights,
stood in the rushy
meadows of my childhood

Or rumbled down lanes,
lumbering before carts.
Tim, the first horse I rode,
seasick on his barrel
back; the first to lip
bread from my hand.

I saw the end of your road.
You stood, with gouged eyeball
while our farmhand swabbed
the hurt socket out with
water and Jeyes Fluid:
as warm an object of

loving memory as any
who have followed me
to this day, denying
rhetoric with your patience,
forcing me to drink
from the trough of reality.

LIKE DOLMENS ROUND MY CHILDHOOD, THE OLD PEOPLE

Like dolmens round my childhood, the old people.

Jamie MacCrystal sang to himself,
A broken song without tune, without words;
He tipped me a penny every pension day,
Fed kindly crusts to winter birds.
When he died, his cottage was robbed,
Mattress and money box torn and searched.
Only the corpse they didn't disturb.

Maggie Owens was surrounded by animals,
A mongrel bitch and shivering pups,
Even in her bedroom a she-goat cried.
She was a well of gossip defiled,
Fanged chronicler of a whole countryside:
Reputed a witch, all I could find
Was her lonely need to deride.

The Nialls lived along a mountain lane
Where heather bells bloomed, clumps of foxglove.
All were blind, with Blind Pension and Wireless,
Dead eyes serpent-flicked as one entered
To shelter from a downpour of mountain rain.
Crickets chirped under the rocking hearthstone
Until the muddy sun shone out again.

Mary Moore lived in a crumbling gatehouse,
Famous as Pisa for its leaning gable.
Bag-apron and boots, she tramped the fields
Driving lean cattle from a miry stable.
A by-word for fierceness, she fell asleep
Over love stories, Red Star and Red Circle,
Dreamed of gypsy love rites, by firelight sealed.

Wild Billy Eagleson married a Catholic servant girl
When all his Loyal family passed on:
We danced round him shouting 'To Hell with King Billy,'
And dodged from the arc of his flailing blackthorn.
Forsaken by both creeds, he showed little concern
Until the Orange drums banged past in the summer
And bowler and sash aggressively shone.

Curate and doctor trudged to attend them,
Through knee-deep snow, through summer heat,
From main road to lane to broken path,
Gulping the mountain air with painful breath.
Sometimes they were found by neighbours,
Silent keepers of a smokeless hearth,
Suddenly cast in the mould of death.

Ancient Ireland, indeed! I was reared by her bedside,
The rune and the chant, evil eye and averted head,
Fomorian fierceness of family and local feud.
Gaunt figures of fear and of friendliness,
For years they trespassed on my dreams,
Until once, in a standing circle of stones,
I felt their shadows pass

Into that dark permanence of ancient forms.

And now, at last, all proud deeds done,
Mouths dust-stopped, dark they embrace
Suitably disposed, as urns, underground.
Cattle munching soft spring grass
— Epicures of shamrock and the four-leaved clover —
Hear a whimper of ancient weapons,
As a whole dormitory of heroes turn over,
Regretting their butchers' days.
This valley cradles their archaic madness
As once, on an impossibly epic morning,
It upheld their savage stride:
To bagpiped battle marching,
Wolfhounds, lean as models,
At their urgent heels.

'God save our shadowed lands
Stalked by this night beast of the dead
– Turnip roundness of the skull,
Sockets smouldering in the head –
Will no St. George or Patrick come,
Restore to us our once blessed
And blossoming, now barren home?'

He paused on the threshold,
Clashed his sword of wood,
His swinging lantern on the snow
Threw blood-red circles where he stood;
Herded listeners gaped
Like goslings, as if they understood.

Bold as brass, a battering knight
Came roaring through the door,
Bussed the ladies on his right,
Smashed the devil to the floor.
Justice triumphs on the spot,
With straw, like guts, strewn everywhere:
False Satan struts no more.

Seen in farmhouse darkness,
Two wearing decades ago;
From which I still recall
Their faces like listening animals,
A stormlamp swinging to and fro,
And from those creaking country rhymes,
That purging láment of bad times.

A WELCOMING PARTY

Wie war das möglich?

That final newsreel of the war:
A welcoming party of almost shades
Met us at the cinema door
Clicking what remained of their heels.

From nests of bodies like hatching eggs
Flickered insectlike hands and legs
And rose an ululation, terrible, shy;
Children conjugating the verb 'to die'.

One clamoured mutely of love
From a mouth like a burnt glove;
Others upheld hands bleak as begging bowls
Claiming the small change of our souls.

Some smiled at us as protectors.
Can these bones live?
Our parochial brand of innocence
Was all we had to give.

To be always at the periphery of incident
Gave my childhood its Irish dimension;
Yet doves of mercy, as doves of air,
Can falter here as anywhere.

That long dead Sunday in Armagh
I learned one meaning of total war
And went home to my Christian school
To kick a football through the air.

The landlord's coat is tulip red,
A beacon on the wine-dark moor;
He turns his well-bred foreign devil's face,
While his bailiff trots before.

His furious hooves drum fire from stone,
A beautiful sight when gone;
Contemplation holds the noble horseman
In his high mould of bone.

Not so beautiful the bandy bailiff,
Churlish servant of an alien will:
Behind the hedge a maddened peasant
Poises his shotgun for the kill.

Evening brings the huntsman home,
Blood of pheasants in a bag:
Beside a turfrick the cackling peasant
Cleanses his ancient weapon with a rag.

The fox, evicted from the thicket,
Evades with grace the snuffling hounds:
But a transplanted bailiff, in a feudal paradise,
Patrols for God His private grounds.

POISONED LANDS*

'Four good dogs dead in one night
And a rooster, scaly legs in the air,
Beak in the dust, a terrible sight!'
Behind high weathered walls, his share
Of local lands, the owner skulks
Or leaves in dismal guttering gaps
A trail of broken branches, roots,
Bruised by his mournful rubber boots.

Neighbours sight him as a high hat
Dancing down hedges, a skeletal shape
Night-haloed with whistling bats,
Or silhouetted against cloudy skies,
Coat turned briskly to the nape,
Sou'westered in harsh surmise.

'Children dawdling home from Mass
Chased a bouncing ball and found,
Where he had stood, scorched tufts of grass,
Blighted leaves' – and here the sound
Of rodent gossip sank – 'worse by far,
Dark radiance as though a star
Had disintegrated, a clinging stench
Gutting the substances of earth and air.'

* A sign seen in the Irish countryside which indicates
that poisoned meat has been laid down to destroy predatory
animals.

At night, like baleful shadowed eyes,
His windows show the way to cars
Igniting the dark like fireflies.
Gusts of song and broken glass
Prelude wild triumphal feasts
Climaxed by sacrifice of beasts.

Privileged, I met him on an evening walk,
Inveigled him into casual weather-talk.
'I don't like country people' he said, with a grin.
The winter sunlight halved his mottled chin
And behind, a white notice seemed to swing and say:
'If you too licked grass, you'd be dead to-day.'

WOODTOWN MANOR

for Morris Graves

I

Here the delicate dance of silence,
The quick step of the robin,
The sudden skittering rush of the wren:
Minute essences move in and out of creation
Until the skin of soundlessness forms again.

Part order, part wilderness,
Water creates its cadenced illusion
Of glaucous, fluent growth;
Fins raised, as in a waking dream,
Bright fish probe their painted stream.

Imaginary animals harbour here:
The young fox coiled in its covert,
Bright-eyed and mean, the baby bird:
The heron, like a tilted italic,
Illuminating the gospel of the absurd.

And all the menagerie of the living marvellous:
Stone shape of toad,
Flicker of insect life,
Shift of wind touched grass
As though a blessing spirit stirred.

II

Twin deities hover in Irish air
Reconciling poles of east and west;
The detached and sensual Indian God,
Franciscan dream of gentleness:
Gravity of Georgian manor
Approves, with classic stare,
Their dual disciplines of tenderness.

First, the dodo disappeared,
Leaving a legend of a simpleton's head,
Grotesque nut-cracker nose:
But a rum, a rare old one,
With feathers like old clothes.

The great Auk struck out for St. Kilda's,
Settled with shaggy Highlanders,
Skin divers and such:
Learned the language of oblivion,
Finally lost touch.

Gone also, as Goldsmith noted,
The bird of Nazareth and the lesser tatou,
Beasts of strange pattern and birds past belief:
Even to number their names, like witchcraft,
Affords sensual relief.

Golden-pawed snowman of Everest,
Wildcat of the Grampians,
Bower-bird of Peru:
Stay hidden wherever you are,
The final inventory is after you!

Somewhere on the ultimate scarp
The last monster will watch
With hooded eyes,
While tiny men trek importantly towards him,
Bristling with strange supplies.

Dare I yet confront
that memory? She poses
on a moist hillside or
stalks through the groin
of the woods on Sunday
mornings, an innocently
accomplished huntress,
acorns snapping beneath
                    her feet.

Her hair is chestnut
light over the stained
freedom of a raincoat;
each breast kernel-slight
under unbleached wool:
as I trudge docile
by her flank, I feel
the gravitational pull
                    of love.

And fight back, knowing
gold of her cheekbones,
her honied, naïve speech
drains power from manhood;
yet for years we walk
Enniskerry, Sallygap,
clasped in talk, neither
willing to let the other
          come or go ...

OBSESSION

Once again, the naked girl
Dances on the lawn
Under the alder trees
Smelling of rain
And ringed Saturn leans
His vast ear over the world:

But though everywhere the unseen
(Scurry of feet, scrape of flint)
Are gathering, I cannot
Protest. My tongue
Lies curled in my mouth –
My power of speech is gone.

Thrash of an axle in snow!
Not until the adept faun-
Headed brother approves
Us both from the darkness
Can my functions return.
Like clockwork, I strike and go.

COUNTRY MATTERS

I

They talk of rural innocence but most marriages
Here (or wherever the great middle-
Class morality does not prevail) are arranged
Post factum, products of a warm night,
A scuffle in a ditch, boredom spiced
By curiosity, by casual desire —
That ancient game ...
                              Rarely
That ancient sweetness.

                    In school
Her hair was unstinted as harvest
Inundating her thin shoulderblades
Almost to her waist. As she ran
The boys called and raced after her
Across the schoolyard, repeating her name
Like something they meant. Until she stopped:
Then they dwindled away, in flight
From a silence.

                    But after dark
The farmhands came flocking to her door
Like migrant starlings, to sit by the fireside
Pretending indifference, or hang around outside
Waiting for a chance to call her away
Down the slope, into darkness.

                              Finally,
Of course, she gave in. Flattered,
Lacking shrewdness, lacking a language?

II

By the time she was fourteen she was known
As a 'good thing'. By the time she was sixteen
She had to go to England 'to get rid of it'.
By the time she was eighteen, no one 'decent'
Or 'self-respecting' would touch her:
With her tangle of hair and nervously
Darkened eyes, she looked and spoke like
'A backstreets whure'.
                    Condemnation
Never lacks a language!

III

She married, eventually, some casual
Labourer from the same class as herself
For in the countryside even beauty
Cannot climb stairs. But my eye
Still follows an early vision when
Grace inhabited her slight form;
Though my hesitant need to praise
Has had to wait a sanction
Greater than sour morality's
                    For lack of courage
                    Often equals lack of a language
                    And the word of love is
                    Hardest to say.

All legendary obstacles lay between
Us, the long imaginary plain,
The monstrous ruck of mountains
And, swinging across the night,
Flooding the Sacramento, San Joaquin,
The hissing drift of winter rain.

All day I waited, shifting
Nervously from station to bar
As I saw another train sail
By, the San Francisco Chief or
Golden Gate, water dripping
From great flanged wheels.

At midnight you came, pale
above the negro porter's lamp.
I was too blind with rain
And doubt to speak, but
Reached from the platform
Until our chilled hands met.

You had been travelling for days
With an old lady, who marked
A neat circle on the glass
With her glove, to watch us
Move into the wet darkness
Kissing, still unable to speak.

THAT ROOM

Side by side on the narrow bed
We lay, like chained giants,
Tasting each other's tears, in terror
Of the news which left little to hide
But our two faces that stared
To ritual masks, absurd and flayed.

Rarely in a lifetime comes such news
Shafting knowledge straight to the heart
Making shameless sorrow start –
Not childish tears, querulously vain –
But adult tears that hurt and harm,
Seeping like acid to the bone.

Sound of hooves on the midnight road
Raised a dramatic image to mind:
The Dean riding late to Marley?
But we must suffer the facts of self;
No one endures a similar fate
And no one will ever know

What happened in that room
But when we came to leave
We scrubbed each other's tears
Prepared the usual show. That day
Love's claims made chains of time and place
To bind us together more: equal in adversity.

LOVING REFLECTIONS

I *Amo, ergo sum*

I hold your ash pale
Face in the hollow
Of my hand and warm
It slowly back to life.
As the eyelashes stir
Exposing brown flecked
Pupils, soft with
Belief in my existence,
I make a transference
Of trust, and know
The power of the magician:
My palm begins to glow.

II *The Blow*

Anger subsiding, I could
Still see the fiery mark
Of my fingers dwindle
On your cheek, but
Did not rush to kiss
The spot. Hypocrisy
Is not love's agent,
Though our fierce awareness
Would distort instinct
To stage a mood.

III *Pitch-Dark*

Truths we upturn
Too near the bone;
Shudder of angels
Into grimacing stone:
Whatever hope we
Woke with, gone.
We cannot imagine
A further dawn.
Only the will says —
Soldier on!

My love, while we talked
They removed the roof. Then
They started on the walls,
Panes of glass uprooting
From timber, like teeth.
But you spoke calmly on,
Your example of courtesy
Compelling me to reply.
When we reached the last
Syllable, nearly accepting
Our positions, I saw that
The floorboards were gone:
It was clay we stood upon.

A PRIVATE REASON

As I walked out at Merval with my wife
Both of us sad, for a private reason,
We found the perfect silence for it,
A beech leaf severed, like the last
Living thing in the world, to crease
The terraced snow, as we
Walked out by Merval.

And the long staged melancholy of allées,
Tree succeeding tree, each glazed trunk
Not a single heaven-invoking nakedness
But a clause, a cold commentary
Of branches, gathering to the stripped
Dignity of a sentence, as we
Walked out by Merval.

There is a sad formality in the Gallic dance,
Linking a clumsy calligraphy of footsteps
With imagined princes, absorbing sorrow
In a larger ritual, a lengthening avenue
Of perspectives, the ice-gripped pond
Our only Hall of Mirrors, as we
Walk back from Merval.

A CHOSEN LIGHT

I *11 rue Daguerre*

At night, sometimes, when I cannot sleep
I go to the *atelier* door
And smell the earth of the garden.

It exhales softly,
Especially now, approaching springtime,
When tendrils of green are plaited

Across the humus, desperately frail
In their passage against
The dark, unredeemed parcels of earth.

There is white light on the cobblestones
And in the apartment house opposite –
All four floors – silence.

In that stillness – soft but luminously exact,
A chosen light – I notice that
The tips of the lately grafted cherry-tree

Are a firm and lacquered black.

II *Salute, in passing*

The voyagers we cannot follow
Are the most haunting. That face
Time has worn to a fastidious mask
Chides me, as one strict master
Steps through the Luxembourg.
Surrounded by children, lovers,
His thoughts are rigorous as trees
Reduced by winter. While the water

Parts for tiny white-rigged yachts
He plots an icy human mathematics —
Proving what content sighs when all
Is lost, what wit flares from nothingness:
His handsome hawk head is sacrificial
As he weathers to how man now is.

III *Radiometers in the rue Jacob*

In the twin
Or triple crystalline spheres
The tiny fans of mica flash;
Snow fleeing on dark ground.

I imagine
One on an executive's desk
Whirling above the memoranda
Or by his mistress's bed

(next to the milk-white telephone)

A minute wind-
Mill casting its pale light
Over unhappiness, ceaselessly
Elaborating its signals

Not of help, but of neutral energy.

for John MacGahern

At times I see it, present
    As a bright day, or a hill,
The only way of saying something
    Luminously as possible.

Not the accumulated richness
    Of an old historical language –
That musk-deep odour!
    But a slow exactness

Which recreates experience
    By ritualizing its details –
Pale web of curtain, width
    Of deal table, till all

Takes on a witch-bright glow
    And even the clock on the mantel
Moves its hands in a fierce delight
    Of so, and so, and so.

HILL FIELD

All that bone bright winter's day
He completed my angle of sight
Patterning the hill field
With snaky furrows,
The tractor chimney smoking
Like his pipe, under the felt hat.

Ten years ago, it was a team
With bulky harness and sucking step
That changed our hill:
Grasping the cold metal
The tremble of the earth
Seemed to flow into one's hands.

Still the dark birds shape
Away as he approaches
To sink with a hovering
Fury of open beaks —
Starling, magpie, crow ride
A gunmetal sheen of gaping earth.

May, and the air is light
On eye, on hand. As I take
The mountain road, my former step
Doubles mine, driving cattle
To the upland fields. Between
Shelving ditches of whitethorn
They sway their burdensome
Bodies, tempted at each turn
By hollows of sweet grass,
Pale clover, while memory,
A restive sally-switch, flicks
Across their backs.
                        The well
Is still there, a half-way mark
Between two cottages, opposite
The gate into Danaghy's field,
But above the protective dry-
Stone rim, the plaiting thorns
Have not been bill-hooked back
And a thick *glaur** floats.
No need to rush to head off
The cattle from sinking soft
Muzzles into leaf smelling
Spring water.
                        From the farm
Nearby, I hear a yard tap gush
And a collie bark, to check
My presence. Our farmhands
Lived there, wife and children
In twin white-washed cells,
A zinc roof burning in summer.
Now there is a kitchen extension
With radio aerial, rough outhouses
For coal and tractor. A housewife
Smiles good-day as I step through
The fluff and dust of her walled

glaur: a thick scum or ooze.

Farmyard, solicited by raw-necked
Stalking turkeys
                    to where cart
Ruts shape the ridge of a valley,
One of many among the switch-
Back hills of what old chroniclers
Called the Star Bog. Uncurling
Fern, white scut of bogcotton,
Spars of bleached bog fir jutting
From heather, make a landscape
So light in wash it must be learnt
Day by day, in shifting detail.
'I like to look across', said
Barney Horisk, leaning on his *slean,* *
'And think of all the people
'Who have bin.'
                    Shards
Of a lost culture, the slopes
Are strewn with cabins, emptied
In my lifetime. Here the older
People sheltered, the Blind Nialls,
Big Ellen, who had been a Fair-
Day prostitute. The bushes cramp
To the evening wind as I reach
The road's end. Jamie MacCrystal
Lived in the final cottage,
A trim grove of mountain ash
Soughing protection round his walls
And bright painted gate. The thatch
Has slumped in, white dust of nettles
On the flags. Only the shed remains
In use for calves, although fuchsia
Bleeds by the wall, and someone
Has propped a yellow cartwheel
Against the door.

slean: a flanged turf spade.

RETURN

From the bedroom you can see
straight to the fringe of the woods
with a cross staved gate to re-
enter childhood's world:
                            the pines
wait, dripping.

              Crumbling black-
berries, seized from a rack
of rusty leaves, maroon tents
of mushroom, pillars uprooting
with a dusty snap;

                  as the bucket
fills, a bird strikes from the bushes
and the cleats of your rubber boot crush
a yellow snail's shell to a smear
on the grass
              (while the wind starts
the carrion smell of the dead fox
staked as warning).

                  Seeing your former
self saunter up the garden path
afterwards, would you flinch,
acknowledging
                  that sensuality,
that innocence?

Jimmy Drummond used bad language at school
All the four-letter words, like a drip from a drain.
At six he knew how little children were born
As well he might, since his mother bore nine,
Six after her soldier husband left for the wars

Under the motto of the Royal Irish, *Clear the Way!*
When his body returned from England
The authorities told them not to unscrew the lid
To see the remnants of Fusilier Drummond inside –
A chancey hand-grenade had left nothing to hide

And Jimmy's mother was pregnant at the graveside –
Clear the way, and nothing to hide.
Love came to her punctually each springtime,
Settled in the ditch under some labouring man:
'It comes over you, you have to lie down.'

Her only revenge on her hasty lovers
Was to call each child after its father,
Which the locals admired, and seeing her saunter
To collect the pension of her soldier husband
Trailed by her army of baby Irregulars.

Some of whom made soldiers for future wars
Some supplied factories in England.
Jimmy Drummond was the eldest but died younger than any
When he fell from a scaffolding in Coventry
Condemned, like all his family, to *Clear the Way!*

Halting in Dungannon between trains
We often wandered outside town
To see the camp where German
Prisoners were kept. A moist litter
Of woodshavings showed
Ground hastily cleared, and then —

The huge parallelogram
Of barbed wire, nakedly measured
And enclosed like a football field
With the guard towers rising, aloof
As goalposts, at either end.

Given length and breadth we knew
The surface area the prisoners paced
As one hung socks to dry outside
His Nissen hut, another tried
To hum and whistle *Lili Marlene*:
They seemed to us much the same

As other adults, except in their
Neutral dress, and finding it normal
To suffer our gaze, like animals,
As we squatted and pried, for an hour
Or more, about their human zoo

Before it was time for shopfronts,
Chugging train, Vincentian school.
A small incident, soon submerged
In our own brisk, bell-dominated rule;
Until, years later, I saw another camp –
Rudshofen in the fragrant Vosges –

Similar, but with local improvements:
The stockade where the difficult knelt,
The laboratory for minor experiments,
The crematorium for Jews and Gypsies
Under four elegant pine towers, like minarets.

This low-pitched style seeks exactness
Decided not to betray the event.
But as I write, the grid of barbed
Wire rises abruptly around me
The smell of woodshavings plugs
My nostrils, a carrion stench.

On the frost held
field, Orpheus
strides, his greaves
bleak with light,
the split lyre
silver hard
in his hands;
sleek after him
the damp-tongued
cringing hounds.

An unaccountable
desire to kneel,
to pray, pulls
my hands but
his head is not
a crown of thorns:
a great antlered
stag, pity
shrinks from
those horns.

FORGE

The whole shed smelt of dead iron:
the dented teeth of a harrow,
the feminine pathos of donkey's shoes.

A labourer backed in a Clydesdale.
Hugely fretful, its nostrils dilated
while the smith viced a hoof

in his apron, wrestling it
to calmness, as he sheared the pith
like wood-chips, to a rough circle.

Then the bellows sang in the tall chimney
waking the sleeping metal, to leap
on the anvil. As I was slowly

beaten to a matching curve
the walls echoed the stress
of the verb *to forge*.

The donkey sat down on the roadside
Suddenly, as though tired of carrying
His cross. There was a varnish
Of sweat on his coat, and a fly
On his left ear. The tinker
Beating him finally gave in,
Sat on the grass himself, prying
His coat for his pipe. The donkey
(not beautiful but more fragile
than any swan, with his small
front hooves folded under him)
Gathered enough courage to raise
That fearsome head, lipping a daisy,
As if to say — slowly, contentedly —
Yes, there is a virtue in movement,
But only going so far, so fast,
Sucking the sweet grass of stubbornness.

for Sean O'Riada

Again, that note! A weaving
melancholy, like a bird crossing
moorland;
          pale ice on a corrie
opening inward, soundless harp-
strings of rain:
              the pathos
of last letters in the 1916 Room
'Mother, I thank ...'
                   a podgy landmine,
Pearse's swordstick leading to a care-
fully profiled picture.
                That point
where folk and art meet, murmurs
Herr Doktor as
             the wail of tin
whistle climbs against fiddle, and
the *bodhran** begins —
              lost cry
of the yellow bittern!

bodhran: a goatskin drum.

BEYOND THE LISS*

for Robert Duncan

Sean the hunchback, sadly
Walking the road at evening
Hears an errant music,
Clear, strange, beautiful,

And thrusts his moon face
Over the wet hedge
To spy a ring of noble
Figures dancing, with —

A rose at the centre —
The lustrous princess.

Humbly he pleads to join,
Saying, 'pardon my ugliness,
Reward my patience,
Heavenly governess.'

Presto! like the frog prince
His hump grows feather
Light, his back splits,
And he steps forth, shining

Into the world of ideal
Movement where (stripped
Of stale selfishness,
Curdled envy) all

liss: a fairy mound or fort.

Act not as they are
But might wish to be —
Planets assumed in
A sidereal harmony —

Strawfoot Sean
Limber as any.

But slowly old habits
Reassert themselves, he
Quarrels with pure gift,
Declares the boredom

Of a perfect music,
And, with goatish nastiness,
Seeks first to insult,
Then rape, the elegant princess.

Presto! with a sound
Like a rusty tearing
He finds himself lifted
Again through the air

To land, sprawling,
Outside the hedge,
His satchel hump securely
Back on his back.

Sean the hunchback, sadly
Walking the road at evening

THE SIEGE OF MULLINGAR, 1963

At the Fleadh Cheoil* in Mullingar
There were two sounds, the breaking
Of glass, and the background pulse
Of music. Young girls roamed
The streets with eager faces,
Shoving for men. Bottles in
Hand, they rowed out a song:
Puritan Ireland's dead and gone,
A myth of O'Connor and O'Faolain.

In the early morning the lovers
Lay on both sides of the canal
Listening on Sony transistors
To the agony of Pope John.
Yet it didn't seem strange, or blasphemous,
This ground bass of death and
Resurrection, as we strolled along:
Puritan Ireland's dead and gone,
A myth of O'Connor and O'Faolain.

Further on, breasting the wind
Waves of the deserted grain harbour
We saw a pair, a cob and his pen,
Most nobly linked. Everything then
In our casual morning vision
Seemed to flow in one direction,
Line simple as a song:
Puritan Ireland's dead and gone,
A myth of O'Connor and O'Faolain.

* A feast or festival of traditional music.

My uncle played the fiddle – more elegantly the violin –
A favourite at barn and cross-roads dance,
He knew *The Sailor's Bonnet* and *The Fowling Piece.*

Bachelor head of a house full of sisters,
Runner of poor racehorses, spendthrift,
He left for the New World in an old disgrace.

He left his fiddle in the rafters
When he sailed, never played afterwards;
A rural art silenced in the discord of Brooklyn.

A heavily-built man, tranquil-eyed as an ox,
He ran a wild speakeasy, and died of it.
During the depression many dossed in his cellar.

I attended his funeral in the Church of the Redemption,
Then, unexpected successor, reversed time
To return where he had been born.

During my schooldays the fiddle rusted
(The bridge fell away, the catgut snapped)
Reduced to a plaything stinking of stale rosin.

The country people asked if I also had music
(All the family had had) but the fiddle was in pieces
And the rafters remade, before I discovered my craft.

Twenty years afterwards, I saw the church again,
And promised to remember my burly godfather
And his rural craft, after this fashion:

So succession passes, through strangest hands.

By the crumbling fire we talked
Animal-dazed by the heat
While the lawyer unhooked a lamp
From peat blackened rafters
And climbed the circle of stairs.

Without, the cattle, heavy for milking,
Shuddered and breathed in the byre.
'It falls early these nights' I said
Lifting tongs to bruise a turf
And hide the sound of argument upstairs

From an old man, hands clenched
On rosary beads, and a hawthorn stick
For hammering the floor —
A nuisance in the working daytime,
But now, signing a parchment,

Suddenly important again, as long before.
Cannily aware of his final scene too,
With bald head swinging like a stone
In irresistible statement: 'It's rightly theirs'
Or: 'They'll never see stick of mine.'

Down in the kitchen, husband and wife
Watched white ash form on the hearth,
Nervously sharing my cigarettes,
While the child wailed in the pram
And a slow dark overcame fields and farm.

When the wall between her and ghost
Wears thin, then snuff, spittoon,
Soothing drink cannot restrain:
She ransacks the empty house.
The latch creaks with the voice
Of a husband, the crab of death
Set in his bowels, even the soft moon
Caught in the bathroom window
Is a grieving woman, her mother
Searching for home in the Asylum.
What awaits, she no longer fears
As dawn paints in the few trees
Of her landscape, a rusty shed
And garden. Today grandchildren
Call, but what has she to say
To the buoyant living, who may
Raise family secrets with the dead?

My father, the least happy
man I have known. His face
retained the pallor
of those who work underground:
the lost years in Brooklyn
listening to a subway
shudder the earth.

But a traditional Irishman
who (released from his grille
in the Clark St. I.R.T.)
drank neat whiskey until
he reached the only element
he felt at home in
any longer: brute oblivion.

And yet picked himself
up, most mornings,
to march down the street
extending his smile
to all sides of the good
(non-negro) neighbourhood
belled by St. Teresa's church.

When he came back
we walked together
across fields of Garvaghey
to see hawthorn on the summer
hedges, as though
he had never left;
a bend of the road

which still sheltered
primroses. But we
did not smile in
the shared complicity
of a dream, for when
weary Odysseus returns
Telemachus must leave.

Often as I descend
into subway or underground
I see his bald head behind
the bars of the small booth;
the mark of an old car
accident beating on his
ghostly forehead.

All afternoon we assemble, a cluster
of children, grand-children, great-
grand-children, in-laws like myself
come to celebrate this scant haired
talkative old lady's
long delaying action against death.

While technicians scurry to arrange
cables, and test for sound,
calmly on the lawn we dispose
ourselves; spokes of a wheel
radiating from that strict centre
where she holds her ground.

Skull cap like a Rembrandt Jew
jowls weathered past yellow to old gold,
the hands in her lap discreetly folded
shelter a black Morocco purse
containing (so the awed family claim)
a sound portfolio from the Paris *bourse*.

As the cameras whir she recites
her life, with the frightening babble
of the age-liberated, entirely free:
how she knew the young Hussar captain
loved her, as passing her window
every morning, he lifted his képi:

how she drove through French and enemy lines
to recover her handsome cavalier son
buried in No Man's Land:
but the hasty planks of her home
made coffin were too short:
his boot gave way in her hand.

She does not raise her failing eyes
to heaven, to attest what she has undergone,
but treats Him like a gentleman
who will know how things are done
when she is finally gathered upwards
with, but not like, everyone ...

THE TRUE SONG

The first temptation is to descend
Into beauty, those lonely waters
Where the swan weeps, and the lady
Waits, a nacreous skeleton.

The second is to watch over
Oneself, a detached god
Whose artifice reflects
The gentle smile in the mirror.

The third, and the hardest,
Is to see the body brought in
From the street, and know
The hand surge towards blessing.

For somewhere in all this
Stands the true self, seeking
To speak, who is at once
Swan
        lady
                stricken one.

PREMONITION

I

The darkness comes slowly alight.
That flow of red hair I recognise
Over the knob of the shoulder
Down your pale, freckled skin,
The breasts I have never seen;
But slowly the line of the tresses
Begins to stir, a movement

That is not hair, but blood
Flowing. Someone is cutting
Your naked body up:
Strapped in dream helplessness
I hear each thrust of the knife
Till that rising, descending blade
Seems the final meaning of life.

Mutely, you writhe and turn
In tremors of ghostly pain,
But I am lost to intervene,
Blood, like a scarlet curtain,
Swinging across the brain
Till the light switches off –
And silence is darkness again.

II

On the butcher's block
Of the operating theatre
You open your eyes.
Far away, I fall back
Towards sleep, the Liffey
Begins to rise, and knock
Against the quay walls

The gulls curve and scream
Over the Four Courts, over
This ancient creaking house
Where, released from dream,
I lie in a narrow room;
Low-ceilinged as a coffin
The dawn prises open.

TIDES

The window blown
open, that summer
night, a full moon

occupying the sky
with a pressure of
underwater light

a pale radiance
glossing the titles
behind your head

& the rectangle
of the bed where,
after long separation,

we begin to make
love quietly, bodies
turning like fish

in obedience to
the pull & tug
of your great tides.

KING & QUEEN

Jagged head
of warrior, bird
of prey, surveying space

side by side
they squat, the pale
deities of this place

giant arms
slant to the calm
of lap, kneebone;

blunt fingers
splay to caress
a rain-hollowed stone

towards which
the landscape of five parishes
tends, band after band

of terminal,
peewit haunted,
cropless bogland.

TO CEASE

for Samuel Beckett

To cease
to be human.

To be
a rock down
which rain pours,
a granite jaw
slowly discoloured.

Or a statue
sporting a giant's beard
of verdigris or rust
in some forgotten
village square.

A tree worn
by the prevailing winds
to a diagram of
tangled branches:
gnarled, sapless, alone.

To cease
to be human
and let birds soil
your skull, animals rest
in the crook of your arm.

To become
an object, honoured
or not, as the occasion demands;
while time bends you slowly
back to the ground.

THE HAG OF BEARE

from the ninth-century Irish

Ebb tide has come for me:
My life drifts downwards
Like a retreating sea
With no tidal turn.

I am the Hag of Beare,
Fine petticoats I used to wear,
Today, gaunt with poverty,
I hunt for rags to cover me.

Girls nowadays
Dream only of money —
When we were young
We cared more for our men.

Riding over their lands
We remember how, like gentlemen,
They treated us well;
Courted, but didn't tell.

Today every upstart
Is a master of graft;
Skinflint, yet sure to boast
Of being a lavish host.

But I bless my King who gave —
Balanced briefly on time's wave —
Largesse of speedy chariots
And champion thoroughbreds.

These arms, now bony, thin
And useless to younger men,
Once caressed with skill
The limbs of princes!

Sadly my body seeks to join
Them soon in their dark home –
When God wishes to claim it,
He can have back his deposit.

No more love-teasing
For me, no wedding feast:
Scant grey hair is best
Shadowed by a veil.

Why should I care?
Many's the bright scarf
Adorned my hair in the days
When I drank with the gentry.

So God be praised
That I misspent my days!
Whether the plunge be bold
Or timid, the blood runs cold.

After spring and autumn
Come age's frost and body's chill:
Even in bright sunlight
I carry my shawl.

Lovely the mantle of green
Our Lord spreads on the hillside!
Every spring the divine craftsman
Plumps its worn fleece.

But my cloak is mottled with age –
No, I'm beginning to dote –
It's only grey hair straggling
Over my skin, a lichened oak.

And my right eye has been taken away
As down payment on heaven's estate;
Likewise the ray in the left
That I may grope to heaven's gate.

No storm has overthrown
The royal standing stone.
Every year the fertile plain
Bears its crop of yellow grain.

But I, who feasted royally
By candlelight, now pray
In this darkened oratory.
Instead of heady mead

And wine, high on the bench
With kings, I sup whey
In a nest of hags:
God pity me!

Yet may this cup of whey
O! Lord, serve as my ale-feast –
Fathoming its bitterness
I'll learn that you know best.

Alas, I cannot
Again sail youth's sea;
The days of my beauty
Are departed, and desire spent.

I hear the fierce cry of the wave
Whipped by the wintry wind.
No one will visit me today
Neither nobleman nor slave.

I hear their phantom oars
As ceaselessly they row
And row to the chill ford,
Or fall asleep by its side.

Flood tide
And the ebb dwindling on the sand!
What the flood rides ashore
The ebb snatches from your hand.

Flood tide
And the sucking ebb to follow!
Both I have come to know
Pouring down my body.

Flood tide
Has not yet rifled my pantry
But a chill hand has been laid
On many who in darkness visited me.

Well might the Son of Mary
Take their place under my roof-tree
For if I lack other hospitality
I never say 'No' to anybody –

Man being of all
Creatures the most miserable –
His flooding pride always seen
But never his tidal turn.

Happy the island in mid-ocean
Washed by the returning flood
But my ageing blood
Slows to final ebb.

I have hardly a dwelling
Today, on this earth.
Where once was life's flood
All is ebb.

A CHARM

When you step near
I feel the dark hood
Descend, a shadow
Upon my mind.

One thing to do,
Describe a circle
Around, about me,
Over, against you:

The hood is still there
But my pupils burn
Through the harsh folds.
You may return

Only as I wish.
But how my talons
Ache for the knob
Of your wrist!

COATLICUE

Your body is small,
squat, deformed as
a Nahautl Indian,
an Aztec image
of necessary death:

casually born
of the swirl of
a river, tossed
up by tides —
sexual flotsam —

regard those swart
small breasts that
will never give milk
though around inflamed
nipples, love-bites

multiply like scars.
Salt wind of desire
upon the flesh!
Black hair swings
over your shoulders

as you bear darkness
down toward me, and
across the sun-robed
pyramid, obsidian knives
resume their sacrifice.

You think I am brutal and without pity but at least I execute cleanly because, like any true killer, I wish to spare the victim. There are worse deaths. I have seen the wounded bird trail her wing, and attract only the scavenger. 'Help me' he croaks as he hops near. One dart of her beak would settle him, for he is only a pale disciple of Death, whom he follows at a distance. But she needs sympathy and when he calls 'I am more unhappy than you' her womanly heart revives and she takes him under her broken wing. Her eyesight is poor and her senses dulled but she feels an echo of lost happiness as he stirs against her breast. She does not realise that he is quietly settling down to his favourite meal of dying flesh, happily enveloped in the smell of incipient putrefaction. The pain grows and spreads through her entire body until she cries aloud but it is too late to shake off his implanted beak. He grinds contentedly on and, as she falls aside, his bony head shoots up, like a scaldy out of a nest. His eye is alert, his veins coursing with another's blood, and for a brief moment, as he steps across the plain without looking back, his tread is firm as a conqueror's.

Again she appears,
The putrid fleshed woman
Whose breath is ashes,
Hair a writhing net of snakes!
Her presence strikes gashes
Of light into the skull
Rears the genitals

Tears away all
I had so carefully built –
Position, marriage, fame –
As heavily she glides towards me
Rehearsing the letters of my name
As if tracing them from
A rain streaked stone.

All night we turn
Towards an unsounded rhythm
Deeper, more fluent than breathing.
In the pale light of morning
Her body relaxes: the hiss of seed
Into that mawlike womb
Is the whimper of death being born.

SPECIAL DELIVERY

The spider's web
of your handwriting
on a blue envelope

brings up too much
to bear, old sea-sick-
ness of love, retch

of sentiment, night
& day devoured by
the worm of delight

which turns to
feed upon itself;
emotion running so

wildly to seed
between us until
it assumes a third

a ghost or child's
face, the soft skull
pale as an eggshell

& the life-cord
of the emerging body —
fish, reptile, bird —

which trails
like the cable
of an astronaut

as we whirl & turn
in our bubble of
blood & sperm

before the gravities
of earth claim us
from limitless space.

        * * *

Now, light years later
your nostalgic letter
admitting failure,

claiming forgiveness.
When fire pales to
so faint an ash

so frail a design
why measure guilt
your fault or mine:

but blood seeps where
I sign before tearing
down the perforated line.

In the Stadsmuzeum at Bruges, there is a picture by Gerard David of a man being flayed. Four craftsmen are concerned with the figure on the table: one is opening the left arm, another lifting away the right nipple, a third incising the right arm while the last (his knife caught between his teeth) is unwinding the results of his labour so as to display the rich network of veins under the skin of the left leg. The only expression in the faces of those looking on is a mild admiration: the Burgmeister has caught up the white folds of his ermine gown and is gazing into the middle distance. It is difficult even to say that there is any expression on the face of the victim, although his teeth are gritted and the cords attaching his wrists to the legs of the table are stretched tight. The whole scene may be intended as an allegory of human suffering but what the line of perspective leads us to admire is the brown calfskin of the principal executioner's boots.

The infinite softness
& complexity of a body
in repose. The hinge

of the ankle bone de-
fines the flat space
of a foot, its puckered

flesh & almost arch.
The calf's heavy curve
sweeping down against

the bony shin, or up
to the warm bulges &
hollows of the knee

describes a line of
gravity, energy as
from shoulder knob

to knuckle, the arm
cascades, round the
elbow, over the wrist.

The whole body a system
of checks & balances –
those natural shapes

a sculptor celebrates,
sea-worn caves, pools,
boulders, tree-trunks –

      or, at every hand's turn,
      a crop of temptation:
      arm & thigh opening

on softer, more secret
areas, hair sprouting
crevices, odorous nooks

& crannies of love,
awaiting the impress
of desire, a fervent

homage, or tempting
to an extinction of
burrowing blindness.

(Deviously uncurling
from the hot clothes
of shame, a desert

father's dream of
sluttish nakedness,
demon with inflamed

breasts, dangling
tresses to drag man
down to hell's gaping

vaginal mouth.)

> To see the model
> as simply human
>
> a mild housewife
> earning pocket money
> for husband & child
>
> is to feel the dark
> centuries peel away
> to the innocence of

the white track on
her shoulders where
above brown flesh

the brassiere lifts
to show the quiet of
unsunned breasts &

to mourn & cherish
each melancholy proof
of mortality's grudge

against perfection:
the appendix scar
lacing the stomach

the pale stitches on
the wailing wall of
the rib-cage where

the heart obediently
pumps.

What homage
is worthy for such

a gentle unveiling?
To nibble her ten
toes, in an ecstasy

of love, to drink
hair, like water?
(Fashion designers

would flatten her
breasts, level the
curves of arse &

stomach, moulding
the mother lode
that pulses beneath

to a uniformity
of robot bliss.)

On cartridge paper

an army of pencils
deploy silently to
lure her into their

net of lines while
from & above her
chilled, cramped

body blossoms
a late flower:
her tired smile.

Silence
& damp night air
Flowing from the garden
Like a young girl
Dissatisfied with
Her mythic burden
Ceres, corn goddess
Mistress of summer,
Steps sure-footed over
The sweet smelling
Bundles of grass.
Her abundant body is
Compounded of honey
& gold, the spike
Of each small nipple
A wild strawberry —
Fulfilled in
Spite of herself
She exchanges with
The moon the pale
Gold disc of her face.

THE SAME GESTURE

There is a secret room
of golden light where
everything – love, violence,
hatred is possible;
and, again love.

Such intimacy of hand
and mind is achieved
under its healing light
that the shifting of
hands is a rite

like court music.
We barely know our
selves there though
it is what we always were
– most nakedly are –

and must remember
when we leave, re-
suming our habits
with our clothes:
work, 'phone, drive

through late traffic
changing gears with
the same gesture as
eased your snowbound
heart and flesh.

LOVE, A GREETING

Love, a greeting
in the night, a
passing kindness,
wet leaf smell
of hair, skin

or a lifetime's
struggle to exchange
with the strange
thing inhabiting
a woman —
                    face,
breasts, buttocks,
the honey sac
of the cunt —

luring us to forget,
beget, a form of truth
or (the last rhyme
tolls its half tone)
an answer to death.

LAST JOURNEY

I.M. James Montague

We stand together
on the windy platform;
how crisp the rails
running out of sight
through the wet fields!

Carney, the station master,
is peering over
his frosted window:
the hand of the signal
points down.

Crowned with churns
a cart creaks up the
incline of Main Street
to the sliding doors
of the Co-Op.

A smell of coal,
the train is coming ...
you climb slowly in,
propped by my hand to
a seat, back to the engine,

and we leave, waving
a plume of black smoke
over the rushy meadows,
small hills & hidden villages –
Beragh, Carrickmore,

Pomeroy, Fintona –
placenames that sigh
like a pressed melodeon
across this forgotten
Northern landscape.

What a view he has
of our town, riding
inland, the seagull!

Rows of shining roofs
and cars, the dome of
a church, or a bald-

headed farmer, and
a thousand gutters
flowing under the

black assembly
of chimneys! If
he misses anything

it might be history
(the ivy-strangled
O'Neill Tower only

a warm shelter to
come to roost if
crows don't land

first, squabbling;
and a planter's
late Georgian house

with its artificial
lake, and avenue of
poplars, less than

the green cloth of
our gold-course where
fat worms hide from

the sensible shoes
of lady golfers).
Or religion. He may

not recognise who
is driving to Mass
with his army of

freckled children –
my elder brother –
or hear Eustace

hammer and plane
a new coffin for
an old citizen,

swearing there is
no one God as the
chips fly downward!

He would be lost,
my seagull, to see
why the names on

one side of the street
(MacAteer, Carney)
are Irish and ours

and the names across
(Carnew, MacCrea)
are English and theirs

but he would understand
the charred, sad stump
of the factory chimney

which will never burn
his tail feathers as
he perches on it

and if a procession,
Orange or Hibernian,
came stepping through

he would hear the
same thin, scrannel
note, under the drums.

And when my mother
pokes her nose out
once, up and down

the narrow street,
and retires inside,
like the lady in

the weather clock,
he might well see
her point. There are

few pickings here,
for a seagull, so
far inland. A last

salute on the flag
pole of the British
Legion Hut, and he

flaps away, the
small town sinking
into its caul

of wet, too well
hedged, hillocky
Tyrone grassland.

Nothing is ever still.
Descend into the harsh
Emerald of the sea depths.
Frond and mollusc,
Coral and seahorse,
Surely this balletic lull
Is the final nursery
Of sway in silence
Where fish break the
Glass of an element
As by magic.
                        But
            Nothing is ever still.
            The crab's metallic arm
            Creaks from the stone
            The transparent shrimp
            Scuttles beneath rain-
            Bow shoals, fleeing before
            The curving predators,
            Part of the slow, perpetual
            Fall of small things
            Down to the rising
            Aggregate of the seabed.
                        Die or devour! But
                        Everything dies into birth
                        On the clambering vacuum
                        Of the sea floor, something
                        Grows, begins to spread
                        A ceaseless, blind
                        Flickering, rain
                        Turning to snow
                        Drifting to sleet,
                        A veil of movement
                        That accumulates, melts
                        Into one relentlessly
                        Converging lathe of power-
                        ful motion: the menace
                        of the undertow!

SEA CHANGES

Each rock pool a garden
Of colour, bronze and
Blue gleam of Irish moss,
Rose of coral algae,
Ochre of sponge where
Whelk and starfish turn
In an odour of low tide;
Faint odour of stillness.

WINE DARK SEA

For there is no sea
it is all a dream
there is no sea
except in the tangle
of our minds:
the wine dark
sea of history
on which we all turn
turn and thresh
       and disappear.

PART II

THE LEAPING FIRE

i.m. Brigid Montague (1876-1966)

Each morning, from the corner
of the hearth, I saw a miracle
as you sifted the smoored ashes
to blow
      a fire's sleeping remains
back to life, holding the burning brands
of turf, between work hardened hands.
I draw on that fire....

I

Old lady, I now celebrate
to whom I owe so much;
bending over me in darkness
a scaly tenderness of touch

skin of bony arm & elbow
sandpapered with work:
because things be to be done
and simplicity did not shirk

the helpless, hopeless task
of maintaining a family farm,
which meant, by legal fiction,
maintaining a family name.

The thongless man's boots,
the shapeless bag apron:
would your favourite saint
accept the harness of humiliation

you bore constantly until
the hiss of milk into the pail
became as lonely a prayer as
your vigil at the altar rail.

Roses showering from heaven
upon Her uncorrupted body
after death, celebrated
the Little Flower's sanctity

& through the latticed grill
of your patron's enclosed order
an old French nun once threw me
a tiny sack of lavender.

So from the pressed herbs
of your least memory, sweetness exudes:
that of the meek and the selfless,
who should be comforted.

II

Nightly she climbs the
narrow length of the stairs
to kneel in her cold room
as if she would storm
heaven with her prayers

which, if they have power,
now reach across the quiet
night of death to where
instead of a worn rosary,
I tell these metal keys.

The pain of a whole family
she gathers into her hands:
the pale mother who died
to give birth to children
scattered to the four winds

who now creakingly arouse
from darkness, distance
to populate the corners
of this silent house
they once knew so well.

A draught whipped candle
magnifies her shadow –
a frail body grown monstrous,
sighing in a trance
before the gilt crucifix –

& as the light gutters
the shadows gather to dance
on the wall of the next room
where, a schoolboy searching sleep,
I begin to touch myself.

The sap of another generation
fingering through a broken tree
to push fresh branches
towards a further light,
a different identity.

III

Your white hair
on the thin rack
of your shoulders

it is hard to
look into the eyes
of the dying

who carry away
a part of oneself –
a shared world

& you, whose life
was selflessness,
now die slowly

broken down by
process to a worn
exhausted beauty

the moon in her
last phase, caring
only for herself.

I lean over the
bed but you barely
recognize me &

when an image
forces entry —
Is that John?

Bring me home
you whimper &
I see a house

shaken by traffic
until a fault runs
from roof to base

but your face has
already retired into
the blind, animal

misery of age
paying out your
rosary beads

hands twitching
as you drift
towards nothingness.

IV

Family legend held
that this frail
woman had heard
the banshee's wail

& on the night
she lay dying
I heard a low,
constant crying

over the indifferent
roofs of Paris —
the marsh bittern
or white owl sailing

from its foul
nest of bones
to warn me with
a hollow note

& among autobuses
& taxis, the shrill
paraphernalia of a
swollen city

I crossed myself
from rusty habit
before I realised
why I had done it.

A hollow note.

To learn the massrock's lesson, leave your car,
Descend frost gripped steps to where
A humid moss overlaps the valley floor.
Crisp as a pistol-shot, the winter air
Recalls poor Tagues, folding the nap of their frieze
Under one knee, long suffering as beasts,
But parched for that surviving sign of grace,
The bog-Latin murmur of their priest.
A crude stone oratory, carved by a cousin,
Commemorates the place. For two hundred years
People of our name have sheltered in this glen
But now all have left. A few flowers
Wither on the altar, so I melt a ball of snow
From the hedge into their rusty tin before I go.

LAMENT FOR THE O'NEILLS

The fiddler settles in
to his playing so easily;
rosewood box tucked under chin,
saw of rosined bow
& angle of elbow

that the mind elides
for a while what he plays:
hornpipe or reel to warm
us up well, heel or toecap
twitching in tune

till the sound expands
in the slow climb of a lament.
As by some forest campfire
listeners draw near, to honour
a communal loss

& a shattered procession
of anonymous suffering
files through the brain:
burnt houses, pillaged farms,
a province in flames.

With an intricate
& mournful mastery
the thin bow glides & slides,
assuaging like a bardic poem,
our tribal pain –

Disappearance & death
of a world, as down Lough Swilly
the great ship, encumbered with nobles,
swells its sails for Europe:
The Flight of the Earls.

All around, shards of a lost tradition:
From the Rough Field I went to school
In the Glen of the Hazels. Close by
Was the bishopric of the Golden Stone;
The cairn of Carleton's homesick poem.

Scattered over the hills, tribal
And placenames, uncultivated pearls.
No rock or ruin, dun or dolmen
But showed memory defying cruelty
Through an image-encrusted name.

The heathery gap where the Raparee,
Shane Barnagh, saw his brother die —
On a summer's day the dying sun
Stained its colours to crimson:
So breaks the heart, Brish-mo-Cree.

The whole landscape a manuscript
We had lost the skill to read,
A part of our past disinherited;
But fumbled, like a blind man,
Along the fingertips of instinct.

The last Gaelic speaker in the parish
When I stammered my school Irish
One Sunday after mass, crinkled
A rusty litany of praise:
Tá an Ghaedilg againn arís ...*

* 'We have the Irish again.'

Tír Eoghain : Land of Owen,
Province of the O'Niall;
The ghostly tread of O'Hagan's
Barefoot gallowglasses marching
To merge forces in Dun Geanainn

Push southward to Kinsale!
Loudly the war-cry is swallowed
In swirls of black rain and fog
As Ulster's pride, Elizabeth's foemen,
Founder in a Munster bog.

(Dumb,
bloodied, the severed
head now chokes to
speak another tongue: —

As in
a long suppressed dream,
some stuttering garb-
led ordeal of my own)

An Irish
child weeps at school
repeating its English.
After each mistake

The master
gouges another mark
on the tally stick
hung about its neck

Like a bell
on a cow, a hobble
on a straying goat.
To slur and stumble

In shame
the altered syllables
of your own name:
to stray sadly home

and find
the turf cured width
of your parents' hearth
growing slowly alien:

In cabin
and field, they still
speak the old tongue.
You may greet no one.

To grow
a second tongue, as
harsh a humiliation
as twice to be born.

Decades later
that child's grandchild's
speech stumbles over lost
syllables of an old order.

SOUND OF A WOUND

Who knows
the sound a wound makes?
    Scar tissue
can rend, the old hurt
    tear open as
the torso of the fiddle
    groans to
carry the tune, to carry
    the pain of
a lost (slow herds of cattle
    roving over
soft meadow, dark bogland)
    pastoral rhythm.

I assert
a civilisation died here;
    it trembles
underfoot where I walk these
    small, sad hills:
it rears in my blood stream
    when I hear
a bleat of Saxon condescension;
    Westminster
to hell, it is less than these
    strangely carved
five thousand year resisting stones,
    that lonely cross.

This bitterness
I inherit from my father, the
    swarm of blood
to the brain, the vomit surge
    of race hatred,
the victim seeing the oppressor,
    bold Jacobean
planter, or gadget laden marine,
    who has scatter-
ed his household gods, used
    his people
as servants, flushed his women
    like game.

When I found the swallow's
Nest under the bridge –
Ankle deep in the bog stream,
Traffic drumming overhead –
I was so pleased, I ran
To fetch a school companion
To share the nude fragility
Of the shells, lightly freckled
With colour, in their cradle
Of feathers, twigs, earth.

It was still breast warm
Where I curved in my hand
To count them, one by one
Into his cold palm, a kind
Of trophy or offering. Turn-
Ing my back, to scoop out
The last, I heard him run
Down the echoing hollow
Of the bridge. Splashing
After, I bent tangled in
Bull wire at the bridge's
Mouth, when I saw him take
And break them, one by one
Against a sunlit stone.

For minutes we fought
Standing and falling in
The river's brown spate,
And I would still fight
Though now I can forgive.

To worship or destroy beauty –
That double edge of impulse
I recognise, by which we live;
But also the bitter paradox
Of betraying love to harm,
Then lunging, too late,
With fists, to its defence.

Plan the next move. *Whereabouts?*
Don't forget the case of stout.
Which only means that, dragging
A crate of bottles between us,
A rump parliament of old friends
Spend the lees of the night in
A mountain cottage, swapping
Stories, till cock-crow warns
Then stagger home, drunk as coots,
Through the sleeping countryside.

A gate clangs, I grope against
A tent-fold of darkness until
Eye accepts the animal shape
Of the hedge, the sphere of
Speckled sky, the pale, damp
Fields breathing on either side.
The lane is smoothly tarred
Downhill to the humped bridge
Where I peer uncertainly over,
Lured towards sense by the
Unseen rattle of this mountain
Stream, whose lowland idlings
Define my townland's shape.

I climbed to its source once,
A journey perilous, through
The lifeless, lichened thorn
Of MacCrystal's Glen, a thread
Of water still leading me on
Past stale bog-cuttings, gray
Shapes slumped in rusty bracken.
Littered with fir's white bone:
Stranded mammoths! The water's
Thin music unwinding upwards
Till, high on a ledge of pale
Reeds and heather, I came
Upon a pool of ebony water
Fenced by rocks ...

                    Legend
Declared a monster trout
lived there, so I slipped
A hand under the fringe of
Each slick rock, splitting
The skin of turning froth
To find nothing but that
Wavering pulse leading to
The central heart where
The spring beat, so icy-cold
I shiver now in recollection,
Hearing its brisk, tireless
Movement over the pebbles
Beneath my feet ...
                    Was that
The ancient trout of wisdom
I meant to catch? As I plod
Through the paling darkness
Details emerge, and memory
Warms. Old Danaghy raging
With his stick, to keep our
Cows from a well, that now
Is boarded up, like himself.
Here his son and I robbed a
Bees' nest, kicking the combs
Free; our boots smelt sweetly
For days afterwards. Snowdrop
In March, primrose in April,
Whitethorn in May, cardinal's
Fingers of foxglove dangling
All summer: every crevice held
A secret sweetness. Remembering,
I seem to smell wild honey
On my face.

And plunge
Down the hillside, singing
In a mood of fierce elation.
My seven league boots devour
Time and space as I crash
Through the last pools of
Darkness. All around, my
Neighbours sleep, but I am
In possession of their past
(The pattern history weaves
From one small backward place)
Marching through memory magnified:
Each grassblade bends with
Translucent beads of moisture
And the bird of total meaning
Stirs upon its hidden branch.

As I reach the last lap
The seventh sense of drunkenness –
That extra pilot in the head –
Tells me I am being watched
And wheeling, I confront a clump
Of bullocks. Inert in grass,
They gaze at me, saucer-eyed,
Turning their slow surprise
Upon their tongue. *Store cattle*:
The abattoirs of old England
Will soon put paid to them. In
A far meadow, the corncrake
turns its rusty ratchet and
I find myself rounding the
Last corner towards the black
Liquid gleam of the main road.

𝕷𝖔𝖘𝖘

Item: The shearing away of an old barn
      criss-cross of beams where pigeons moan
      high small window where the swallow built
      white-washed dry-stone walls.

Item: The suppression of stone lined paths
      old potato-boiler full of crocuses
      overhanging lilac or laburnum
      sweet pea climbing the fence.

Item: The filling-in of chance streams
      uncovered wells, all unchannelled sources
      of water that might weaken foundations
      bubbling over the macadam.

Item: The disappearance of all signs
      of wild life, wren's or robin's nest,
      a rabbit nibbling a coltsfoot leaf,
      a stray squirrel or water rat.

Item: The uprooting of wayside hedges
      with their accomplices, devil's bit and pee the bed,
      prim rose and dog rose, an unlawful
      assembly of thistles.

Item: The removal of all hillocks
      and humps, superstition styled fairy forts
      and long barrows, now legally to be regarded
      as obstacles masking a driver's view.

* from 'Hymn to the New Omagh Road'.

Gain

Item: 10 men from the district being for a period of time
fully employed, their ten wives could buy groceries
and clothes to send 30 children content to school for a
few months, and raise local merchants' hearts by
paying their bills.

Item: A man driving from Belfast to Londonderry can
arrive a quarter of an hour earlier, a lorry load of
goods ditto, thus making Ulster more competitive
in the international market.

Item: A local travelling from the prefabricated suburbs of
bypassed villages can manage an average of 50
rather than 40 miles p.h. on his way to see relatives in
Omagh hospital or lunatic asylum.

Item: The dead of Garvaghey Graveyard (including my
grandfather) can have an unobstructed view – the trees
having been sheared away for a carpark – of the living
passing at great speed, sometimes quick enough to
come straight in:

Let it be clear
That I do not grudge my grandfather
This long delayed pleasure!
I like the idea of him
Rising from the rotting boards of the coffin
With his J.P.'s white beard
And penalising drivers
For travelling faster
Than jaunting cars

for Bernadette Devlin

Once again, it happens.
Under a barrage of stones
and flaring petrol bombs
the blunt, squat shape of
an armoured car glides
into the narrow streets
of the Catholic quarter
leading a file of helmet-
ed, shielded riot police;
once again, it happens,
like an old Troubles film,
run for the last time ...

Lines of history
   lines of power
the long sweep
   of the Bogside
under the walls
   up to Creggan
the black muzzle
   of Roaring Meg
staring dead on
   cramped houses
the jackal shapes
   of James's army
watching the city
   stiffen in siege

SMALL SHOT HATH
   POURED LIKE HAIL
THE GREAT GUNS
   SHAKEN OUR WALLS
a spectral garrison
   no children left
sick from eating
   horseflesh, vermin
curs fattened on
   the slain Irish
still flaunting
   the bloody flag
of 'No Surrender'
GOD HAS MADE US
AN IRON PILLAR
   AND BRAZEN WALLS
AGAINST THIS LAND.

Lines of defiance
   lines of discord
near the Diamond
   brisk with guns
British soldiers
   patrol the walls
the gates between
   Ulster Catholic
Ulster Protestant
   a Saracen slides
past the Guildhall
   a black Cuchulain
bellowing against
   the Scarlet Whore
twin races petrified
   the volcanic ash
of religious hatred

symbol of Ulster
   these sloping streets
blackened walls
   sick at heart and
seeking a sign
   the flaghung gloom
of St. Columb's
   the brass eagle of
the lectern bearing
   the Sermon on the Mount
in its shoulders
   'A city that is
set on a hill
   cannot be hid.'

Columba's Derry!
   ledge of angels
radiant oakwood
   where the man dove
knelt to master
   his fiery temper
exile chastened
   the bright candle
of the Uí Néill
   burns from Iona
lightens Scotland
   with beehive huts
glittering manuscripts
   but he remembers
his secret name
   'He who set his
back on Ireland.'

Lines of leaving
   lines of returning
the long estuary
   of Lough Foyle, a
ship motionless
   in wet darkness
mournfully hooting
   as a tender creeps
to carry passengers
   back to Ireland
a child of four
   this sad sea city
my landing place
   the loneliness of
Lir's white daughter's
   ice crusted wings
forever spread
   at the harbour mouth.

Rearing westward
   the great sunroom
of Inis Eoghain
   coiling stones of
Aileach's hillfort
   higher than Tara
the Hy Niall
   dominating Uladh
the white cone
   of Sliabh Snacht
sorrow veiled
   the silent fjord
*is uaigneach Eire**
   as history's wind
plucks a dynasty
   from the ramparts
bids a rival
   settlement rise

* Ireland is lonely

121

London's Derry!
  METHOUGHT I SAW
DIDOE'S COLONY
  BUILDING OF CARTHAGE*
culverin and saker
  line strong walls
but local chiefs
  come raging in
O'Cahan, O'Doherty
  (a Ferrara sword
his visiting card)
  a New Plantation
a new mythology
  Lundy slides
down a peartree
  as drum and fife
trill ORANJE BOVEN!

Lines of suffering
  lines of defeat
under the walls
  ghetto terraces
sharp pallor of
  unemployed shades
slope shouldered
  broken bottles
pubs and bookies
  red brick walls
Falls or Shankhill
  Lecky or Fountain
love's alleyway
  message scrawled
Popehead: Tague
  my own name
hatred's synonym

But will the meek
inherit the earth?
  RELIGION POISONS US
NORTH AND SOUTH,
  A SPECIAL FORCE OF
ANGELS WE'D NEED
  TO PUT MANNERS ON US.
IF THE YOUNG WERE
  HONEST, THEY'D ADMIT
THEY DON'T HOLD
  WITH THE HALF OF IT.
THE SHOWBANDS
  AND THE BORDER HALLS
THAT'S THE STUFF
  Said the guardian
of the empty church
  pale siege windows
shining behind us

Lines of protest
  lines of change
a drum beating
  across Berkeley
all that Spring
  invoking the new
Christ avatar
  of the Americas
running voices
  streets of Berlin
Paris, Chicago
  seismic waves
zigzagging through
  a faulty world

* Sir John Davies

Overflowing from
  narrow streets
cramped fields
    a pressure rising
to match it
  tired marchers
    nearing Burntollet
    young arms linked
banners poled high
    the baptism of
flying missiles
    spiked clubs
Law and Order's
    medieval armour
of glass shield
    and dangling baton

Lines of action
    lines of reaction
the white elephant
    of Stormont, Carson's
raised right claw
  a Protestant parliament
a Protestant people
  major this and
captain that and
  general nothing
the bland, pleasant
    face of mediocrity
confronting in horror
    its mirror image
bull-voiced bigotry

the emerging order
    of the poem invaded
by cries, protestations
    a people's pain
the defiant face
    of a young girl
campaigning against
    memory's mortmain
a blue banner
    lifting over a
broken province
    DRIVE YOUR PLOUGH
a yellow bulldozer
    raising the rubble
a humming factory
    a housing estate
hatreds sealed into
    a hygienic honeycomb

Lines of loss
    lines of energy
always changing
    always returning
A TIDE LIFTS
    THE RELIEF SHIP
OFF THE MUD
    OVER THE BOOM
the rough field
    of the universe
growing, changing
    a net of energies
crossing patterns
    weaving towards
a new order
    a new anarchy
always different
    always the same

I

I go to say goodbye to the *Cailleach**
that terrible figure who haunted my childhood
but no longer harsh, a human being
merely, hurt by event.

               The cottage,
circled by trees, weathered to admonitory
shapes of desolation by the mountain winds,
straggles into view. The rank thistles
and leathery bracken of untilled fields
stretch behind with – a final outcrop –
the hooped figure by the roadside,
its retinue of dogs

                    which give tongue
as I approach, with savage, whining cries
so that she slowly turns, a moving nest
of shawls and rags, to view, to stare
the stranger down.

                And I feel again
that ancient awe, the terror of a child
before the great hooked nose, the cheeks
dewlapped with dirt, the staring blue
of the sunken eyes, the mottled claws
clutching a stick

               but now hold
and return her gaze, to greet her,
as she greets me, in friendliness.
Memories have wrought reconciliation
between us, we talk in ease at last,
like old friends, lovers almost,
sharing secrets

*Cailleach: Irish and Scots Gaelic for an old woman, a hag

of neighbours
she quarrelled with, who now lie
in Garvaghey graveyard, beyond all hatred;
of my family and hers, how she never married,
though a man came asking in her youth
'You would be loath to leave your own'
she sighs, 'and go among strangers' —
his parish ten miles off.

For sixty years
since she has lived alone, in one place.
Obscurely honoured by such confidences,
I idle by the summer roadside, listening,
while the monologue falters, continues,
rehearsing the small events of her life.
The only true madness is loneliness,
the monotonous voice in the skull
that never stops
                because never heard.

II

And there
where the dog rose shines in the hedge
she tells me a story so terrible
that I try to push it away,
my bones melting.

Late at night
a drunk came beating at her door
to break it in, the bold snapping
from the soft wood, the thin mongrels
rushing to cut, but yelping as
he whirls with his farm boots
to crush their skulls.

                    In the darkness
they wrestle, two creatures crazed
with loneliness, the smell of the
decaying cottage in his nostrils
like a drug, his body heavy on hers,
the tasteless trunk of a seventy year
old virgin, which he rummages while
she battles for life

                    bony fingers
reaching desperately to push
against his bull neck. 'I prayed
to the Blessed Virgin herself
for help and after a time
I broke his grip.'

                    He rolls
to the floor, snores asleep,
while she cowers until dawn
and the dogs' whimpering starts
him awake, to lurch back across
the wet bog.

    III

                    And still
the dog rose shines in the hedge.
Petals beaten wide by rain, it
sways slightly, at the tip of a
slender, tangled, arching branch
which, with her stick, she gathers
into us.

                    'The wild rose
is the only rose without thorns,'
she says, holding a wet blossom
for a second, in a hand knotted
as the knob of her stick.
'Whenever I see it, I remember
the Holy Mother of God and
all she suffered.'

                    Briefly
the air is strong with the smell
of that weak flower, offering
its crumbled yellow cup
and pale bleeding lips
fading to white

                              at the rim
of each bruised and heart-
shaped petal.

FOR THE HILLMOTHER

Hinge of silence
          creak for us
Rose of darkness
          unfold for us
Wood anemone
          sway for us
Blue harebell
          bend to us
Moist fern
          unfurl for us
Springy moss
          uphold us
Branch of pleasure
          lean on us
Leaves of delight
          murmur for us
Odorous wood
          breathe on us
Evening dews
          pearl for us
Freshet of ease
          flow for us
Secret waterfall
          pour for us
Hidden cleft
          speak to us
Portal of delight
          inflame us
Hill of motherhood
          wait for us
Gate of birth
          open for us

MAD SWEENY

A wet silence.
Wait under trees,
muscles tense,
ear lifted, eye alert.

Lungs clear.
A nest of senses
stirring awake –
human beast!

A bird lights:
two claw prints.
Two leaves shift:
a small wind.

Beneath, white
rush of current,
stone chattering
between high banks.

Occasional shrill
of a bird, squirrel
trampolining along
a springy branch.

Start a slow
dance, lifting
a foot, planting
a heel to celebrate

greenness, rain
spatter on skin,
the humid pull
of the earth.

The whole world
turning in wet
and silence, a
damp mill wheel.

In silence and isolation, the dance begins. No one is meant to watch, least of all yourself. Hands fall to the sides, the head lolls, empty, a broken stalk. The shoes fall away from the feet, the clothes peel away from the skin; body rags. The sight has slowly faded from your eyes, that sight of habit which sees nothing. Your ears buzz a little before they retreat to where the heart pulses, a soft drum. Then the dance begins, cleansing, healing. Through the bare forehead, along the bones of the feet, the earth begins to speak. One knee lifts rustily, then the other. Totally absent, you shuffle up and down, the purse of your loins striking against your thighs, sperm and urine oozing down your lower body like a gum. From where the legs join the rhythm spreads upwards – the branch of the penis lifting, the cage of the ribs whistling – to pass down the arms like electricity along a wire. On the skin moisture forms, a wet leaf or a windbreath light as a mayfly. In wet and darkness you are reborn, the rain falling on your face as it would on a mossy tree trunk, wet hair clinging to your skull like bark, your breath mingling with the exhalations of the earth, that eternal smell of humus and mould.

MESSAGE

With a body
heavy as earth
she begins to speak;

her words
are dew, bright
deadly to drink

her hair
the damp mare's
nest of the grass

her arms,
thighs, chance
of a swaying branch

her secret
message, shaped
by a wandering wind

puts the eye
of reason out;
so novice, blind,

ease your
hand into the
rot smelling crotch

of a hollow
tree, and find
two pebbles of quartz

protected by
a spider's web:
her sunless breasts.

SESKILGREEN

A circle of stones
surviving behind a
guttery farmhouse,

the capstone phallic
in a thistly meadow:
Seskilgreen Passage Grave.

Cup, circle,
triangle beating
their secret dance

(eyes, breasts,
thighs of a still
fragrant goddess).

I came last in May
to find the mound
drowned in bluebells

with a fearless wren
hoarding speckled eggs
within a stony crevice

while cattle
swayed sleepily
under low branches

lashing the ropes
of their tails
across the centuries.

WINDHARP

for Patrick Collins

The sounds of Ireland,
that restless whispering
you never get away
from, seeping out of
low bushes and grass,
heatherbells and fern,
wrinkling bog pools,
scraping tree branches,
light hunting cloud,
sound hounding sight,
a hand ceaselessly
combing and stroking
the landscape, till
the valley gleams
like the pile upon
a mountain pony's coat.

DOWAGER

I dwell in this leaky Western castle.
American matrons weave across the carpet,
Sorefooted as camels, and less useful.

Smooth Ionic columns hold up a roof.
A chandelier shines on a foxhound's coat:
The grandson of a grandmother I reared.

In the old days I read or embroidered,
But now it is enough to see the sky change,
Clouds extend or smother a mountain's shape.

Wet afternoons I ride in the Rolls;
Windshield wipers flail helpless against the rain:
I thrash through pools like smashing panes of glass.

And the light afterwards! Hedges steam,
I ride through a damp tunnel of sweetness,
The bonnet strewn with bridal hawthorn

From which a silver lady leaps, always young.
Alone, I hum with satisfaction in the sun,
An old bitch, with a warm mouthful of game.

COURTYARD IN WINTER

Snow curls in on the cold wind.

Slowly, I push back the door.
After long absence, old habits
Are painfully revived, those disciplines
Which enable us to survive,
To keep a minimal fury alive
While flake by faltering flake

Snow curls in on the cold wind.

Along the courtyard, the boss
Of each cobblestone is rimmed
In white, with winter's weight
Pressing, like a silver shield,
On all the small plots of earth,
Inert in their living death as

Snow curls in on the cold wind.

Seized in a giant fist of frost,
The grounded planes at London Airport,
Mallarmé swans, trapped in ice.
The friend whom I have just left
Will be dead, a year from now
Through her own fault, while

Snow curls in on the cold wind.

Or smothered by some glacial truth?
Thirty years ago, I learnt to reach
Across the rusting hoops of steel
That bound our greening waterbarrel
To save the living water beneath
The hardening crust of ice, before

Snow curls in on the cold wind.

But despair has a deeper crust.
In all our hours together, I never
Managed to ease the single hurt
That edged her towards her death;
Never reached through her loneliness
To save a trust, chilled after

Snow curls in on the cold wind.

I plunged through snowdrifts once,
Above our home, to carry
A telegram to a mountain farm.
Fearful but inviting, they waved me
To warm myself at the flaring
Hearth before I faced again where

Snow curls in on the cold wind.

The news I brought was sadness.
In a far city, someone of their name
Lay dying. The tracks of foxes,
Wild birds as I climbed down
Seemed to form a secret writing
Minute and frail as life when

Snow curls in on the cold wind.

Sometimes, I know that message.
There is a disease called snow-sickness;
The glare from the bright god,
The earth's reply. As if that
Ceaseless, glittering light was
All the truth we'd left after

Snow curls in on the cold wind.

So, before dawn, comfort fails.
I imagine her end, in some sad
Bedsitting room, the steady hiss
Of the gas more welcome than an
Act of friendship, the protective
Oblivion of a lover's caress if

Snow curls in on the cold wind.

In the canyon of the street
The dark snowclouds hesitate,
Turning to slush almost before
They cross the taut canvas of
The street stalls, the bustle
Of a sweeper's brush after

Snow curls in on the cold wind.

The walls are spectral, white.
All the trees black-ribbed, bare.
Only veins of ivy, the sturdy
Laurel with its waxen leaves,
Its scant red berries, survive
To form a winter wreath as

Snow curls in on the cold wind.

* * *

What solace but endurance, kindness?
Against her choice, I still affirm
That nothing dies, that even from
Such bitter failure memory grows;
The snowflake's structure, fragile
But intricate as the rose when

Snow curls in on the cold wind.

SMALL SECRETS

Where I work
out of doors
children come
to present me
with an acorn
a pine cone —
small secrets —

and a fat
grass snail
who uncoils
to carry his
whorled house
over the top
of my table.

With a pencil
I nudge him
back into
himself, but
fluid horns
unfurl, damp
tentacles, to

probe, test
space before
he drags his
habitation
forward again
on his single
muscular foot

rippling along
its liquid self-
creating path.
With absorbed,
animal faces
the children
watch us both

but he will
have none of
me, the static
angular world
of books, papers —
which is neither
green nor moist —

only to climb
around, over
as with rest-
less glistening
energy, he races
at full tilt
over the ledge

onto the grass.
All I am left
with is, between
pine cone & acorn
the silver smear
of his progress
which will soon

wear off, like
the silvery galaxies,
mother of pearl
motorways, woven
across the grass
each morning by
the tireless snails

of the world,
minute as grains
of rice, gross
as conch or
triton, bequeath-
ing their shells
to the earth.

We match paces along the Hill Head Road,
the road to the old churchyard of Errigal Keerogue;
its early cross, a heavy stone hidden in grass.

As we climb, my old Protestant neighbour
signals landmarks along his well trodden path,
some hill or valley celebrated in local myth.

'Yonder's Whiskey Hollow', he declares,
indicating a line of lunar birches.
We halt to imagine men plotting

against the wind, feeding the fire or
smothering the fumes of an old fashioned worm
while the secret liquid bubbles & clears.

'And that's Foxhole Brae under there — '
pointing to the torn face of a quarry.
'It used to be crawling with them.'

(A red quarry slinks through the heather,
a movement swift as a bird's, melting as rain,
glimpsed behind a mound, disappears again.)

At Fairy Thorn Height the view fans out,
ruck and rise to where, swathed in mist
& rain, swells the mysterious saddle shape

of Knockmany Hill, its brooding tumulus
opening perspectives beyond our Christian myth.
'On a clear day you can see far into Monaghan,'

old Eagleson says, and we exchange sad notes
about the violence plaguing these parts;
last week, a gun battle outside Aughnacloy,

machine gun fire splintering the wet thorns,
two men beaten up near dark Altamuskin,
an attempt to blow up Omagh Courthouse.

Helicopters overhead, hovering locusts.
Heavily booted soldiers probing vehicles, streets,
their strange antennae bristling, like insects.

At his lane's end, he turns to face me.
'Tell them down South that old neighbours
can still speak to each other around here'

& gives me his hand, but does not ask me in.
Rain misting my coat, I turn back towards
the main road, where cars whip smartly past

between small farms, fading back into forest.
Soon all our shared landscape will be effaced,
a quick stubble of pine recovering most.

VIEWS

I *Back Door*

Oh, the wet melancholy
of morning fields! We
wake to a silence more
heavy than twilight
where an old car finds
its last life as a henhouse
then falls apart slowly
before our eyes, dwindling
to a rust-gnawed fender
where a moulting hen
sits, one eye unlidding;
a mystic of vacancy.

II *Kerry*

Shapes of pine and cypress
shade the hollow where
on thundery nights
facing uphill, the
cattle sleep. Blossoms
of fuchsia and yellow whin
drift slowly down upon
their fragrant, cumbersome
backs. Saga queens,
they sigh, knees
hidden in a carpet
of gold, flecked with
blue and scarlet.

THE CAVE OF NIGHT

for Sean Lucy

Men who believe in absurdities
will commit atrocities.   (Voltaire)

   I *Underside*

I have seen the high
vapour trails of the last
destroyers in dream:
I have seen the grey
underside of the moon
slide closer to earth ...

   II *The Plain of Adoration*
      from the Irish, eleventh century

Here was raised
a tall idol of savage fights:
the Cromm Cruaich –
the King Idol of Erin.

He was their Moloch,
this withered hump of mists,
hulking over every path,
refusing the eternal kingdom.

In a circle stood
four times three idols of stone:
to bitterly enslave his people,
the pivot figure was of gold.

In dark November,
when the two worlds near each other,
he glittered among his subjects,
blood-crusted, insatiable.

To him, without glory,
would they sacrifice their first-born:

with wailing and danger
pouring fresh blood for the Stooped One.

Under his shadow
they cried and mutilated their bodies:
from this worship of dolour
it is called the Plain of Adoration.

Well born Gaels lay prostrate
beneath his crooked shape until
gross and glittering as a cinema organ
he sank back into his earth.

III *Cave*

The rifled honeycomb
of the high-rise hotel
where a wind tunnel moans.
While jungleclad troops
ransack the Falls, race
through huddled streets,
we lie awake, the wide
window washed with rain,
your oval face, and tide
of yellow hair luminous
as you turn to me again
seeking refuge as the
cave of night blooms
with fresh explosions.

IV *All Night*

All night spider webs
of nothing. Condemned to
that treadmill of helplessness.
Distended, drowning fish,
frogs with lions' jaws.
A woman breasted butterfly
copulates with a dying bat.

A pomegranate bursts slowly
between her ladyship's legs.
Her young peep out
with bared teeth:
the eggs of hell
fertilizing the abyss.

Frail skyscrapers incline
together like stilts.
Grain elevators melt.
Cities subside as liners
leave by themselves,
all radios playing.
A friendly hand places
a warm bomb under
the community centre
where the last evacuees
are trying a hymn.
Still singing, they
part for limbo, still
tucking their blankets
over separating limbs.

A land I did not seek
to enter. Pure terror.
Ice floes sail past
grandly as battleships.
Blue gashed arctic distances
ache the retina and
the silence grows to
a sparkle of starlight.
Lift up your telescope,
old colonel, and learn
to lurch with the penguins!
In the final place
a solitary being begins
its slow dance....

v *Ratonnade*

Godoi, godoi, godoi!
Our city burns & so did Troy,
Finic, Finic, marshbirds cry
As bricks assemble a new toy.

        Godoi, etc.

Humble mousewives crouch in caves,
Monster rats lash their tails,
Cheese grows scarce in Kingdom Come,
Rodents leap to sound of drum.

        Godoi, etc.

Civilisation slips & slides when
Death sails past with ballroom glide:
Tangomaster of the skulls whose
Harvest lies in griefs & rues.

        Godoi, etc.

On small hillsides darkens fire,
Wheel goes up, forgetting tyre,
Grudgery holds its winter court,
Smash and smithereens to report.

        Godoi, etc.

Against such horrors hold a cry,
Sweetness mothers us to die,
Nicens digs its garden patch,
Silence lifts a silver latch.

        Godoi, etc.

Mingle musk love-birds say,
Honey-hiving all the day,
Ears & lips & private parts,
Muffled as the sound of carts.

Godoi, etc.

Moral is of worsens hours,
Cripple twisting only flowers,
One arm lost, one leg found,
Sad men fall on common ground.

Godoi!

1972

He was pulled out, squealing,
an iron cleek sunk in the roof
of his mouth.

(Don't say they are not intelligent:
they know the hour has come
and they want none of it;
they dig in their little trotters,
will not go dumb or singing
to the slaughter.)

That high pitched final effort,
no single sound could match it –
a big plane roaring off,
a *diva* soaring towards her last note,
the brain-chilling persistence of an electric saw,
scrap being crushed.

Piercing & absolute,
only high heaven ignores it.

Then a full stop.
An expert plants
a solid thump of a mallet
flat between the ears.

Swiftly the knife seeks the throat;
swiftly the other cleavers work
till the carcass is hung up
shining and eviscerated as
a surgeon's coat.

A child is given the bladder to play with.
But the walls of the farmyard still
hold that scream, are built around it.

THE MASSACRE

Two crows flap to a winter wood.
Soldiers with lances and swords
Probe the entrails of innocents.
A burgomeister washes manicured
Hands before mourning citizens.
The snow on the gable is linen crisp,
That on the ground laced with blood.
Two crows flap to a winter wood.

BORDER LAKE

The farther North you travel, the colder it gets.
Take that border county of which no one speaks.
Look at the scraggly length of its capital town:
the bleakness after a fair, cattle beaten home.
The only beauty nearby is a small glacial lake
sheltering between drumlin moons of mountains.
In winter it is completely frozen over, reeds
bayonet sharp, under a low, comfortless sky.
Near the middle, there is a sluggish channel
where a stray current tugs to free itself.
The solitary pair of swans who haunt the lake
have found it out, and come zigzagging
holding their breasts aloof from the jagged
edges of large pale mirrors of ice.

A GRAVEYARD IN QUEENS

for Eileen Carney

We hesitate along
flower encumbered

avenues of the dead;
Greek, Puerto-Rican,

Italian, Irish —
(our true Catholic

world, a graveyard)
but a squirrel

dances us to it
through the water

sprinklered grass
collapsing wreaths,

& taller than you
by half, lately from

that hidden village
where you were born

I sway with you
in a sad, awkward

dance of pain
over the grave of

my uncle & namesake —
the country fiddler —

& the grave of almost
all your life held,

your husband & son
all three sheltering

under the same
squat, grey stone.

*

You would cry out
against what has

happened, such
heedless hurt,

had you the harsh
nature for it

(swelling the North
wind with groans,

curses, imprecations
against heaven's will)

but your mind is
a humble house, a

soft light burning
beneath the holy

picture, the image
of the seven times

wounded heart of
her, whose portion

is to endure. For
there is no end

to pain, nor of
love to match it

& I remember Anne
meekest of my aunts

rocking & praying
in her empty room.

Oh, the absurdity
of grief in that

doll's house, all
the chair legs sawn

to nurse dead children:
love's museum!

*

It sent me down
to the millstream

to spy upon a
mournful waterhen

shushing her young
along the autumn

flood, as seriously
as a policeman and

after scampering
along, the proud

plumed squirrel
now halts, to stand

at the border
of this grave plot

serious, still,
a small ornament

holding something
a nut, a leaf —

like an offering
inside its paws.

*

For an instant
you smile to see

his antics, then
bend to tidy

flowers, gravel
like any woman

making a bed,
arranging a room,

over what were
your darlings' heads

and far from
our supposed home

I submit again
to stare soberly

at my own name
cut on a gravestone

& hear the creak
of a ghostly fiddle

filter through
American earth

the slow pride
of a lament.

AT LAST

A small sad man with a hat
he came through the customs at Cobh
carrying a roped suitcase and
something in me began to contract

but also to expand. We stood,
his grown sons, seeking for words
which under the clouding mist
turn to clumsy, laughing gestures.

At the mouth of the harbour lay
the squat shape of the liner
hooting farewell, with the waves
striking against Spike Island's grey.

We drove across Ireland that day,
lush river valleys of Cork, russet
of the Central Plain, landscapes
exotic to us Northerners, halting

only in a snug beyond Athlone
to hear a broadcast I had done.
How strange in that cramped room
the disembodied voice, the silence

after, as we looked at each other!
Slowly our eyes managed recognition.
'Well done' he said, raising his glass:
father and son at ease, at last.

'To have gathered from the air a live tradition.' (*Ezra Pound*)

Roving, unsatisfied ghost,
old friend, lean closer;
leave us your skills:
lie still in the quiet
of your chosen earth.

1 *Woodtown Manor, Again*

We vigil by the dying fire,
talk stilled for once,
foil clash of rivalry,
fierce Samurai pretence.

Outside a rustle of bramble,
jack fox around the framing
elegance of a friend's house
we both choose to love:

two natives warming ourselves
at the revived fire
in a high ceilinged room
worthy of Carolan –

clatter of harpsichord
the music leaping
like a long candle flame
to light ancestral faces

pride of music
pride of race

II

Abruptly, closer to self-revelation
than I have ever seen, you speak;
bubbles of unhappiness breaking
the bright surface of *Till Eulenspiegel*.

I am in great danger, you whisper,
as much to the failing fire
as to your friend & listener;
though, *you have great luck.*

Our roles reversed, myself cast
as the light-fingered master,
the lucky dancer on thin ice,
rope walker on his precipice.

III

I sense the magisterial strain
behind your jay's laugh,
ruddy moustached, smiling,
your sharp player's mask.

Instinct wrung and run
awry all day, powers idled
to self-defeat, the vacuum
behind the catalyst's gift.

Beyond the flourish
of personality, peacock
pride of music or language:
a constant, piercing torment!

Signs earlier, a stranger
made to stumble at a bar door,
fatal confusion of the powers
of the upper and lower air.

A playing with fire, leading
you, finally, tempting you
to a malevolence, the
calling of death for another.

IV

A door opens,
and she steps into the room,
smothered in a black gown,
harsh black hair falling to her knees,
a pale tearstained face.

How pretty you look,
Miss Death!

v *Samhain*

Sing a song
for the mistress
of the bones

the player
on the black keys
the darker harmonies

light jig
of shoe buckles
on a coffin lid

* * *

pale glint
of the wrecker's lantern
on a jagged cliff

across the ceaseless
glitter of the spume:
a seagull's creak

the damp haired
seaweed stained sorceress
marshlight of defeat

* * *

chill of winter
a slowly failing fire
faltering desire

Darkness of Darkness
we meet on our way
in loneliness

Blind Carolan
Blind Raftery
Blind Tadgh

VI *Hell Fire Club*

Around the house all night
dark music of the underworld,
hyena howl of the unsatisfied,
latch creak, shutter sigh,
the groan and lash of trees,
a cloud upon the moon.

Released demons moan.
A monstrous black tom
couchant on the roofbeam.
The widowed peacock screams
knowing the fox's tooth:
a cry, like rending silk

& a smell of carrion where
baulked of their prey,
from pane to tall window
pane, they flit, howling
to where he lies, who has
called them from defeat.

Now, their luckless meat,
turning a white pillowed room,
smooth as a bridal suite
into a hospital bed where
a lucid beast fights against
a blithely summoned doom.

At the eye of the storm
a central calm, where
tearstained, a girl child
sleeps cradled in my arms
till the morning points
and you are gone.

VII *The Two Gifts*

And a nation mourns:
The blind horseman with his harp carrying servant,
Hurrying through darkness to a great house
Where a lordly welcome waits, as here:

Fingernail spikes in candlelight recall
A ripple & rush of upland streams,
The slant of rain on void eye sockets,
The shrill of snipe over mountains
Where a few stragglers nest in bracken –
After Kinsale, after Limerick, after Aughrim,
After another defeat, to be redeemed
By the curlew sorrow of an aisling.

The little Black Rose
(To be sprinkled with tears)
The Silk of the Kine
(To be shipped as dead meat)

'They tore out my tongue
So I grew another one.'
I heard a severed head
Sing down a bloody stream.

But a lonelier lady mourns,
the muse of a man's particular gift,
Mozart's impossible marriage of fire & ice,
skull sweetness of the last quartets,
Mahler's horn wakening the autumn forest,
the harsh blood pulse of Stravinsky,
the hammer of Boulez
                    which you will never lift.

Never to be named with your peers,
I am in great danger, he said;
firecastles of flame,
a name extinguished?

   VIII *Lament*

With no family
& no country

a voice rises
out of the threatened beat
of the heart & the brain cells

(not for the broken people
nor for the blood soaked earth)

a voice
like an animal howling
to itself on a hillside
in the empty church of the world

a lament so total
it mourns no one
but the globe itself
turning in the endless halls

of space, populated
with passionless stars

and that always raised voice

TRACKS

I

The vast bedroom
a hall of air,
our linked bodies
lying there.

II

As I turn to kiss
your long, black
hair, small breasts,
heat flares from
your fragrant skin,
your eyes widen as
deeper, more certain
and often, I enter
to search possession
of where your being
hides in flesh.

III

Behind our eyelids
a landscape opens,
a violet horizon
pilgrims labour across,
a sky of colours
that change, explode
a fantail of stars
the mental lightning
of sex illuminating
the walls of the skull;
a floating pleasure dome.

IV

I shall miss you
creaks the mirror
into which the scene
shortly disappears:
the vast bedroom
a hall of air, the
tracks of our bodies
fading there, while
giggling maids push
a trolley of fresh
linen down the corridor.

An ache, anger
thunder of a hurtling
waterfall in the ears:
in abrupt detail he sees
the room where she lays
      her warm, soft body
      under another's

      her petal mouth
      raised to absorb
      his probing kiss
and hears her small voice
      cry animal cries
in the hissing anguish
      the release of

      my sweet one
my darling, my love
until they fall apart
(Oh, the merciless track
of jealousy's film)
      in a wet calm
like flowers after rain.

TALISMAN

After talking together
we move, as by a natural
progress, to make love.
Slant afternoon light

on the bed, the unlatched
window, scattered sheets
are part of a pattern
hastening towards memory

as you give yourself
to me with a cry of
joy, not hunger, while
I receive the gift

in ease, not raw desire
& all the superstructure
of the city outside –
twenty iron floors

of hotel dropping
to where the late sun
strikes the shield of
the lake, its chill towers –

are elements in a slowly
developing dream, a talisman
of calm, to invoke against
unease, to invoke against harm.

DON JUAN'S FAREWELL

Ladies I have lain
        with in darkened rooms
sweet shudder of flesh
        behind shadowy blinds
long bars of light
        across tipped breasts
warm mounds of
        breathing sweetness
young flesh redolent
        of crumpled roses
the tender anxiety
        of the middle-aged
a hovering candle
        hiding blue veins.
eloquent exhaustion
        watching light fade
as your drowsy partner
        drifts towards the
warm shores of sleep
        and you slowly awake
to confront again
        the alluring lie
of searching through
        another's pliant body
for something missing
        in your separate self
while profound night
        like a black swan
goes pluming past.

In the white city of Evora, absence accosted me.
You were reading in bed, while I walked all night alone.
Were you worried about me, or drifting towards sleep?

I saw the temple of Diana, bone white in the moonlight.
I made a private prayer to her, for strength to continue:
Not since convent days have I prayed so earnestly.

A dog came out of the shadows, brushed against my leg.
He followed me everywhere, pushing his nose into my hand.
Soon the cats appeared, little scraggly bundles of need.

There were more monuments, vivid as hallucinations.
Suddenly, a young man stepped out of the shadows:
I was not terrified, as I might have been at home.

Besides, he was smiling & gentle as you used to be.
'A kiss' he pleads 'a kiss' in soft Portuguese.
I quickened my step, but he padded behind me.

He looked so young, my heart went out to him.
I stopped in the shadows under the Cathedral.
We kissed, and the tears poured down my face.

TEARING

I

I sing your pain
as best I can
    seek
like a gentle man
    to assume
the proffered blame.

The pose breaks.
The sour facts remain.
    It takes
two to make or break
    a marriage.
Unhood the falcon!

II *Pastourelle*

Hands on the pommel
long dress trailing
over polished leather
riding boots, a spur
jutting from the heel,
& beneath, the bridle path,
strewn with rusty apples,
brown knobs of chestnut,
meadow saffron and acorn.

Then we were in the high
ribbed dark of the trees
where animals move stealth-
ily, coupling & killing,

while we talked nostalgically
of our lives, bedevilled
& betrayed by lost love —
the furious mole, tunnelling
near us his tiny kingdom —

& how slowly we had come
to where we wished each other
happiness, far and apart, as
a hawk circled the wood,
& a victim cried, the sound
of hooves rising & falling
upon bramble & fern, while
a thin growth of rain gather-
ed about us, like a cowl.

III *Never*

In the gathering dark
I caress your head
as you thrash out
flat words of pain:
'There is no way back,
I can feel it happening;
we shall never be
what we were, again.'

Never, a solemn bell
tolling through
that darkening room
where I cradle your head,
only a glimmer left
in the high window
over what was once
our marriage bed.

SEPARATION

Two fish float:

one slowly downstream
into the warm
currents of the known

the other tugging
against the stream,
disconsolate twin,

the golden
marriage hook
tearing its throat.

NO MUSIC

I'll tell you a sore truth, little understood.
It's harder to leave, than to be left:
To stay, to leave, both sting wrong.

You will always have me to blame,
Can dream we might have sailed on;
From absence's rib, a warm fiction.

To tear up old love by the roots,
To trample on past affections:
There is no music for so harsh a song.

* * *

A blind cripple, trailing
His stick across cobbles;
A butterfly with a torn wing.

Rue Daguerre, how we searched
till we found it! Beyond
the blunt pawed lion of Denfert
to where, after the bustle
of an open stalled market
you halt, before stooping
into a cobbled courtyard.

Symbol of the good life
this silence, each bend-
ing to his chosen task;
a Japanese framer, tire-
less and polite, tending
a grafted cherry tree as
if it were his exiled self

which foamed to brief
and splendid blossom
each European spring.
The florist who made a
speciality of wreaths,
flower woven cartwheels
a cortège on his walls

smothered at Christmas
by fragrant limbs of fir.
The old woman stitching
moleskin sacks and bags
while her gross, gelded
cat dozed towards death
along its sunlit bench.

On Sunday mornings,
white canes racked,
two blind men played
the accordion, those
simple rippling tunes
that tore the heart;
sous les toits de Paris.

Or, *la vie en rose,*
setting for a shared
life, slowly broken,
wrenched, torn apart,
change driving its
blunt wedge through
what seemed permanent:

the cobbles uprooted,
the framer beheaded
in a multiple accident,
a giant tower hulking
over the old market,
the traffic's roar
(waves grinding near

a littered shore)
while time whirls
faster and faster,
*j'attendrai tous
les jours,* a blind
accordion playing
to a funeral wreath.

THE BLUE ROOM

Tired, turning, restless
the insomniac feels the pulse
that feeds his body

pity for his past,
fear of the future,
his spirit beats

along his veins
a ceaseless, dervish dance
which defies oblivion.

Night a pit into
which he falls & falls
endlessly, his memories

a circle of hobbyhorses
grinding up and down
gross, grinning teeth

until dawn biting
its throat, a bird
starts its habitual

terrible, day-beginning cry.
The trees emerge from the stillness.
The raindrop bends the leaf.

SHE DREAMS

Habituée of darkness I have become.
Familiar of the secret feeding grounds
Where terror and dismay ceaselessly hatch,
Black forms curling and uncoiling;
The demons of the night feel like friends.

Something furry brushes along my arm,
A bat or screech owl hurtling by.
I clamber over stained rocks and find
The long gathered contents of our house
Swarming with decay, a filthied nest.

I came to where the eggs lay in the grass.
I watched them for a long time, warming them
With my swollen eyes. One after another
They chipped and scraggy heads appeared;
The embryos of our unborn children.

They turn towards me, croaking 'Mother!'
I gather them up into my apron
But the shape of the house has fallen
And you are asleep by the water's edge:
A wind and wave picked skeleton.

HERBERT STREET REVISITED

for Madeleine

I

A light is burning late
in this Georgian Dublin street:
someone is leading our old lives!

And our black cat scampers again
through the wet grass of the convent garden
upon his masculine errands.

The pubs shut: a released bull,
Behan shoulders up the street,
topples into our basement, roaring 'John!'

A pony and donkey cropped flank
by flank under the trees opposite;
short neck up, long neck down,

as Nurse Mullen knelt by her bedside
to pray for her lost Mayo hills,
the bruised bodies of Easter Volunteers.

Animals, neighbours, treading the pattern
of one time and place into history,
like our early marriage, while

tall windows looked down upon us
from walls flushed light pink or salmon
watching and enduring succession.

II

As I leave, you whisper,
'don't betray our truth'
and like a ghost dancer,
invoking a lost tribal strength
I halt in tree-fed darkness

to summon back our past,
and celebrate a love that eased
so kindly, the dying bone,
enabling the spirit to sing
of old happiness, when alone.

III

So put the leaves back on the tree,
put the tree back in the ground,
let Brendan trundle his corpse down
the street singing, like Molly Malone.

Let the black cat, tiny emissary
of our happiness, streak again
through the darkness, to fall soft
clawed into a landlord's dustbin.

Let Nurse Mullen take the last
train to Westport, and die upright
in her chair, facing a window
warm with the blue slopes of Nephin.

And let the pony and donkey come —
look, someone has left the gate open —
like hobbyhorses linked in
the slow motion of a dream

parading side by side, down
the length of Herbert Street,
rising and falling, lifting
their hooves through the moonlight.

CROSSING

Your lithe & golden body
haunts me, as I haunt you:
corsairs with different freights
who may only cross by chance
    on lucky nights.

So, our moorings differ.
But scents of your pleasure
still linger disturbingly
around me: fair winds or
    squalls of danger?

There is a way of forgetting you.
But I have forgotten it:
prepared wildly to cut free,
to reach, like a young man,
    toward ecstasy!

Nightly your golden body turns
& turns in my shuddering dream.
Why is the heart never still,
yielding again to the cardinal lure
    of the beautiful?

WALKING LATE

Walking late
we share night sounds
so delicate the heart misses
a beat to hear them:

shapes in the half-dark
where the deer feed or
rest, the radar of small
ears & horns still alert
under the glooming boles
of the great oaks
                    to unfold
their knees from the wet grass
with a single thrust & leap away
stiff-legged, in short, jagged
bursts as we approach
                    stars lining
our path through the woods
with a low coiling mist
over the nocturnal meadows
so that we seem to wade
through the filaments
of a giant silver web
the brain crevices of a cloud.

        * * *

Bleached and white
as a fish's belly,
a road curves towards the city
which, with the warming dawn,

will surge towards activity again,
the bubble of the Four Courts
overruling the stagnant quays,
their ghostly Viking prows,

and the echoing archways,
tenebrous walls of the Liberties
where we briefly share a life
to which we must return

as we circle uncertainly
towards a home, your
smaller hand in mine,
trustful, still afraid.

SONG

Let me share with you
a glimpse of richness:
two swans startled me
turning low over the Lee,
looking for a nestling place.
I thought of us, our need
for a place to lay our heads;
our flight secret, unheralded.

By the curl and gleam
of water, my sadness
was washed away:
the air was bright
and clear as your forehead,
the linked swans
reached the wood:
my love, come here to stay.

SUNSET

In Loch Lene
a queen went swimming;
a redgold salmon
flowed into her
at full of evening.

from the *Félire Oengus*

WAITING

Another day of dancing summer,
Evelyn kneels on a rock, breasts
Swollen by approaching motherhood,
Hair bleached by the sea winds
To a pale as honey gold, some
Generous natural image of the good.
Sails butterfly to her nakedness,
Surprised to spy through the haze
A curved figure, sleek as a mermaid,
Or bowsprit Venus, of smooth wood,
Courting the sun and not the shade,
Seagulls aureoling her bowed head,
Translucent as Wicklow river gold;
Source of my present guilt and pride.

CHILD

for Una

A firefly gleams, then
fades upon your cheek.
Now you hide beneath
everything I write;
love's invisible ink,
heart's watermark.

THE POINT

Rocks jagged in morning mist.
At intervals, the foghorn sounds
From the white lighthouse rock
Lonely as cow mourning her calf,
Groaning, belly deep, desperate.

I assisted at such failure once;
A night-long fight to save a calf
Born finally, with broken neck,
It flailed briefly on the straw,
A wide-eyed mother straddling it.

Listen carefully. This is different.
It sounds to guide, not lament.
When the defining light is powerless,
Ships hesitating down the strait
Hear its harsh voice as friendliness.

Upstairs my wife & daughter sleep.
Our two lives have separated now.
But I would send my voice to yours
Cutting through the shrouding mist
Like some friendly signal in distress.

The fog is lifting, slowly.
Flag high, a new ship is entering.
The opposite shore unveils itself,
Bright in detail as a painting,
Alone, but equal to the morning.

EDGE

Edenlike as your name
this sea's edge garden
where we rest, beneath
the clarity of a lighthouse.

To fly into risk,
attempt the dream,
cast off, as we have done,
requires true luck

who know ourselves
blessed to have found
between this harbour's arms
a sheltering home

where the vast
tides of the Atlantic
lift to caress
rose coloured rocks.

So fate relents.
Hushed and calm,
safe and secret,
on the edge is best.

The structure of process,
time's gullet devouring
parents whose children
are swallowed in turn,
families, houses, towns,
built or battered down,
only the earth and sky
unchanging in change,
everything else fragile
as a wild bird's wing;
bulldozer and butterfly,
dogrose and snowflake
climb the unending stair
into God's golden eye.

Everyone close in his own
world of sense & memory,
races, countries closed
in their dream of history,
only love, or friendship,
an absorbing discipline —
the healing harmonies
of music, painting, the poem —
as swaying ropeladders
across fuming oblivion
while the globe turns,
and the stars turn, and
the great circles shine,
gold & silver,
                    sun & moon.

THE WELL DREAMS

I

The well dreams;
liquid bubbles.

Or it stirs
as a water spider skitters across;
a skinny legged dancer.

Sometimes, a gross interruption:
a stone plumps in.
That takes a while to absorb,
to digest, much groaning
and commotion in the well's stomach
before it can proffer again
a nearly sleek surface.

Even a pebble can disturb
that tremor laden miniscus,
that implicit shivering.
They sink towards the floor,
the basement of quiet,
settle into a small mosaic.

And the single eye
of the well dreams on,
a silent cyclops.

II

People are different.
They live outside, insist
in their world of agitation.
A man comes by himself,
singing or in silence,
and hauls up his bucket slowly –
an act of meditation –
or jerks it up angrily,
like lifting a skin,

sweeping a circle
right through his own reflection.

III

And the well recomposes itself.

Crowds come, annually, on pilgrimage.
Votive offerings adorn the bushes;
a child's rattle, hanging silent
(except when the wind touches it)
a rag fluttering like a pennant.

Or a tarnished coin is thrown in,
sinking soundlessly to the bottom.
Water's slow alchemy washes it clean:
a queen of the realm, made virgin again.

IV

Birds chatter above it.
They are the well's principal distraction,
swaying at the end of branches,
singing and swaying, darting excitement
of courting and nesting,
fending for the next brood,
who still seem the same robin,
thrush, blackbird or wren.

The trees stay mainly silent.
The storms speak through them.
Then the leaves come sailing down,
sharp green or yellow,
betraying the seasons,
till a flashing shield of ice
forms over the well's single eye:
the year's final gift,
a static transparence.

V

But a well has its secret.
Under the drifting leaves,
the dormant stones in
the whitewashed wall,
the unpredictable ballet
of waterbugs, insects,

there the spring pulses,
little more than a tremor,
a flickering quiver,
spasms of silence,
small intensities of mirth,
the hidden laughter of earth.

And now, the road towards Cavan.
Each year, we left you down
by the roadside, Mary Mulvey,
to seek out old relations.
We waited, as you hobbled
away, up that summer boreen.

Mary lived in the leaning
cottage, beside the old well
she strove to keep clean,
bending over to skim dead leaves
and insects; ageing guardian
whom we found so frightening

Huddled on the leather seats
of Uncle John's Tin Lizzie
away from your sour, black
shawls, clacking rosary, not
your bag of peppermints, which
we devoured, thoughtlessly.

Maria Marunkey, our hurtful
childish name for your strange
shape, suffering age, its shame
that hooped your back, cramped
and horrible as some toothy witch.
We hammered stones on your roof.

Or hunkered whispering past
your half-door, malefic dwarfs,
to startle your curtained silence
with shouts, coarse as farts:
Maria Marunkey married a donkey.
The latch stirs; we scatter, bravely.

Blessedly, you could barely hear,
or begged us in, with further sweets
or gifts, to share your secret.
Nudging, we thronged around
as you laboriously wound —
more creakingly each year —

The magic music box, resurrected
from camphored lace, which ground
out such light, regular sounds,
thawing ice, tinkling raindrops,
a small figure on its rosewood top
twirling slowly, timeless dancer.

By its grace, I still remember
you, Mary Mulvey, hobbling along
a summer lane, bent over the well
or shuffling into your cottage,
its gable sideways, like yourself.
Your visits to the home place

To see old friends and neighbours
stopped one year when you were
too crippled to move, and besides;
'There's no one left up there.
They've all died off.' A silver
dancer halts. Silent. Motionless.

I

The eagle looked at this changing world;
sighed and disappeared into the mountain.

Before he left he had a last reconnoitre:
the multi-coloured boats in the harbour

Nodded their masts, and a sandy white
crescent of strand smiled back at him.

How he liked the slight, drunk lurch
of the fishing fleet, the tide hoist-

ing them a little, at their ropes' end.
Beyond, wrack, and the jutting rocks

emerging, slowly, monsters stained
and slimed with strands of seaweed.

Ashore, beached boats and lobster
pots, settled as hens in the sand.

II

Content was life in its easiest form;
another was the sudden, growling storm

which the brooding eagle preferred
bending his huge wings into the winds'

wild buffeting, or thrusting down along
the wide sky, at an angle, slideways to

survey the boats, scurrying homewards,
tacking against the now contrary winds,

all of whom he knew by their names.
To be angry in the morning, calmed

by midday, but brooding again in
the evening was all in a day's quirk

with lengthy intervals for silence,
gliding along, like a blessing, while

the fleet toiled on earnestly beneath
him, bulging with a fine day's catch.

III

But now he had to enter the mountain.
Why? Because a cliff had asked him?
The whole world was changing, with one
language dying, and another encroaching,
bright with buckets, cries of children.
There seemed to be no end to them,
and the region needed a guardian –
so the mountain had told him. And

A different destiny lay before him:
to be the spirit of that mountain.
Everyone would stand in awe of him.
When he was wrapped in the mist's caul
they would withdraw because of him,
peer from behind blind, or curtain.
When he lifted his wide forehead
bold with light, in the morning,
they would all laugh and smile with him.
It was a greater task than an eagle's
aloofness, but sometimes, under his oilskin
of coiled mist, he sighed for lost freedom.

The text around the seal reads: SOCIETY · OF · UNITED · IRISHMEN · BELFAST. On the banner: IT · IS · NEW · STRUNG · AND · SHALL · BE · HEARD.

CONTENTS

PART ONE

PART TWO